South Carolina

Rules of Evidence

Annotated

2019

Daniel M. Coble, Esq.

Printed in the United States of America

First Printing, 2019

ISBN 9781793879646

Everyday Evidence Books
Columbia, SC 29206
www.EverydayEvidence.org

About this book

This book consists of the South Carolina Rules of Evidence. The most commonly used rules contain explanations and case law. The majority of the case law is from the S.C. Supreme Court and the S.C. Court of Appeals.

Contents

Article I. General Provisions

RULE 101
SCOPE

Except as otherwise provided by rule or by statute, these rules govern proceedings in the courts of South Carolina to the extent and with the exceptions stated in Rule 1101.

Note:

This rule differs from the federal rule in two regards. First, the phrase "except as otherwise provided by rule or by statute" is added to make it clear that statutes or other rules promulgated by the Supreme Court may limit the applicability of these rules. An example of such a rule is Rule 11 of the South Carolina Administrative and Procedural Rules for Magistrate's Court which provides that the rules of evidence apply in civil actions before the magistrate's court, but allows those rules to be relaxed in the interest of justice. Second, the phrase "courts of South Carolina" has been substituted for the phrase "courts of the United States, and before the United States bankruptcy judges and United States magistrate judges." Rule 1101 provides greater detail regarding the applicability of these rules in various proceedings.

RULE 102
PURPOSE AND CONSTRUCTION

These rules shall be construed to secure fairness in administration, elimination of unjustifiable expense and delay, and promotion of growth and development of the law of evidence to the end that the truth may be ascertained and proceedings justly determined.

Note:

This rule is identical to the federal rule.

RULE 103
RULINGS ON EVIDENCE

(a) Effect of Erroneous Ruling. Error may not be predicated upon a ruling which admits or excludes evidence unless a substantial right of the party is affected, and

> **(1) Objection.** In case the ruling is one admitting evidence, a timely objection or motion to strike appears of record, stating the specific ground of objection, if the specific ground was not apparent from the context; or

> **(2) Offer of Proof.** In case the ruling is one excluding evidence, the substance of the evidence and the specific evidentiary basis supporting admission were made known to the court by offer or were apparent from the context.

(b) Record of Offer and Ruling. The court may add any other or further statement which shows the character of the evidence, the form in which it was offered, the objection made, and the ruling thereon. It may direct the making of an offer in question and answer form.

(c) Hearing of Jury. In jury cases, proceedings shall be conducted, to the extent practicable, so as to prevent inadmissible evidence from being suggested to the jury by any means, such as making statements or offers of proof or asking questions in the hearing of the jury.

Note:

11

This rule is identical to the federal rule with the exception of the omission of subsection (d) relating to plain error. The rule of plain error contained in the federal rule is inconsistent with the law in South Carolina. Cf. State v. Torrence, 305 S.C. 45, 406 S.E.2d 315 (1991) (abolishing in favorem vitae review in capital cases and holding that error must be preserved by contemporaneous objection in the trial court). It should be noted that the Supreme Court has recognized a very few limited circumstances in which it will review issues raised for the first time on appeal. Cf. Toyota of Florence, Inc. v. Lynch, 314 S.C. 257, 442 S.E.2d 611 (1994) (challenge to abhorrent and outrageous argument raised for first time on appeal); State v. Pace, 316 S.C. 71, 447 S.E.2d 186 (1994) (failure to make contemporaneous objection to judge's comments excused where judge's tone and tenor made it clear that any objection would have been futile). Further, the failure to adopt a rule of plain error in no way limits the authority of trial judges to raise evidentiary issues on their own motion.

Subsection (a) means that reversal on appeal is only required where a substantial right of a party has been affected; error which is harmless does not affect a substantial right. Graham, Handbook of Federal Evidence, 103.1 (3rd ed. 1981). This is equivalent to South Carolina law holding that reversal is not required unless an error is prejudicial and not harmless. State v. Sosebee, 284 S.C. 411, 326 S.E.2d 654 (1985) (probable prejudice must be shown); State v. Gaskins, 284 S.C. 105, 326 S.E.2d 132 (1985) (a new trial is not required for harmless error), cert. denied, 471 U.S. 1120, 105 S.Ct. 2368, 86 L.Ed.2d 266 (1985), overruled on other grounds, State v. Torrence, 305 S.C. 45, 406 S.E.2d 315 (1991); Watts v. Bell Oil Co., 266 S.C. 61, 221 S.E.2d 529 (1976) (prejudice must be shown).

Subsection (a)(1) is generally in accord with prior South Carolina law which required a contemporaneous objection

12

with specific grounds to preserve an error for review. State v.
Hoffman, 312 S.C. 386, 440 S.E.2d 869 (1994)
(contemporaneous objection); White v. Wilbanks, 298 S.C.
225, 379 S.E.2d 298 (Ct. App.1989) (contemporaneous
objection), rev'd on other grounds, 301 S.C. 560, 393 S.E.2d
182 (1990); State v. Bailey, 253 S.C. 304, 170 S.E.2d 376
(1969) (specific grounds required; general objection
preserves nothing). It does somewhat relax the requirement of
stating specific grounds where the grounds are apparent from
the context. The better practice, however, is for counsel to
always give, and the court always to require, specific grounds
for an objection; this will avoid later disputes regarding what
was apparent from the context. It should be noted that Rule
43(i), SCRCP, Rule 18, SCRCrimP, and Rule 9(b), SCRFC,
do not prevent counsel from stating the grounds for an
objection, but merely control argument on the grounds for the
objection. This rule does not alter the prior practice
regarding motions in limine, which allowed the motion to
exclude evidence to be made at the pretrial stage, State v.
Glenn, 285 S.C. 384, 330 S.E.2d 285 (1985), but required a
contemporaneous objection when the evidence is actually
offered into evidence at the trial to preserve the issue for
review. State v. Schumpert, ___ S.C. ____, 435 S.E.2d 859
(1993); Parr v. Gaines, 309 S.C. 477, 424 S.E.2d 515 (Ct.
App.1992).

Subsection (a)(2) is the federal rule modified to require the
grounds for admission to be stated. As modified, this rule is
consistent with South Carolina law which requires a proffer
of the excluded evidence and the grounds for admission to be
stated to preserve the trial court's ruling for review. State v.
Cabbagestalk, 281 S.C. 35, 314 S.E.2d 10 (1984); State v.
Cox, 258 S.C. 114, 187 S.E.2d 525 (1972); Legrande v.
Legrande, 178 S.C. 230, 182 S.E. 432 (1935); Gold Kist, Inc.
v. Citizens & Southern Nat'l Bank, 286 S.C. 272, 333 S.E.2d
67 (Ct. App.1985). The rule does change South Carolina law

by dispensing with the requirement of a proffer and a statement of the grounds for admissibility where the substance of the evidence and the grounds are apparent from the context. The prior law only dispensed with the requirement of a proffer where the judge refused to allow a proffer. State v. Schmidt, 288 S.C. 301, 342 S.E.2d 401 (1986). To avoid later disputes over what was apparent from the context, however, the better practice is for a proffer and a statement of the grounds to always be made.

The first sentence of subsection (b) is similar to language contained in former Rule 43(c), SCRCP. Although no specific South Carolina case can be found to support the second sentence, requiring an offer to be made in question and answer form is within the discretion of the judge.

Subsection (c) is in accord with prior South Carolina law. Chandler v. People's Nat'l Bank, 140 S.C. 433, 138 S.E. 888 (1927); Rule 43(c), SCRCP.

Case Law

"In order to preserve an error for appellate review, a defendant must make a contemporaneous objection on a specific ground. *State v. Hoffman,* 312 S.C. 386, 440 S.E.2d 869 (1994); *State v. Crowley,* 226 S.C. 472, 85 S.E.2d 714 (1955)…'The objection should be sufficiently specific to bring into focus the precise nature of the alleged error so that it can be reasonably understood by the trial judge.' *McKissick v. J.F. Cleckley & Co.,* 325 S.C. 327, 344, 479 S.E.2d 67, 75 (Ct.App.1996)."
State v. Holliday, 333 S.C. 332, 338, 509 S.E.2d 280, 283 (Ct. App. 1998)

"A contemporaneous objection is required to properly preserve an error for appellate review. *State v. Torrence,* 305 S.C. 45, 406 S.E.2d 315 (1991). Here, the record shows that no such preservation occurred. Defense counsel's lone objection was well after the initial admission of the choking incident."
State v. Hoffman, 312 S.C. 386, 393, 440 S.E.2d 869, 873 (1994)

RULE 104
PRELIMINARY QUESTIONS

(a) Questions of Admissibility Generally. Preliminary questions concerning the qualification of a person to be a witness, the existence of a privilege, or the admissibility of evidence shall be determined by the court, subject to the provisions of subdivision (b). In making its determination it is not bound by the rules of evidence except those with respect to privileges.

(b) Relevancy Conditioned on Fact. When the relevancy of evidence depends upon the fulfillment of a condition of fact, the court shall admit it upon, or subject to, the introduction of evidence sufficient to support a finding of the fulfillment of the condition.

(c) Hearing of Jury. Hearings on the admissibility of confessions or statements by an accused, and pretrial identifications of an accused shall in all cases be conducted out of the hearing of the jury. Hearings on other preliminary matters shall be so conducted when the interests of justice require, or when an accused is a witness and so requests.

(d) Testimony by Accused. The accused does not, by testifying upon a preliminary matter, become subject to cross-examination as to other issues in the case.

(e) Weight and Credibility. This rule does not limit the right of a party to introduce before the jury evidence relevant to weight or credibility.

Note:

Except for subsection (c), this rule is identical to the federal rule.

The first sentence of subsection (a) is in accord with prior South Carolina law. Wright v. Pub. Sav. Life Ins. Co., 262 S.C. 285, 204 S.E.2d 57 (1974). No South Carolina authority has been found which specifically determines whether a judge must apply the rules of evidence in conducting a hearing on the admissibility of evidence. Cf. Congdon v. Morgan, 14 S.C. 587 (1880) (passing comment that judge did not violate rules of evidence during hearing on admissibility of evidence).

Subsection (b) addresses situations where the relevancy of an item of evidence depends upon the existence of a particular preliminary fact. Prior South Carolina case law has recognized that a judge commits no error in admitting evidence where its relevancy is established later in the trial. Perry v. Jefferies, 61 S.C. 292, 39 S.E. 515 (1901) (evidence of acts of defendant's agents admitted before any evidence of agency introduced).

Subsection (c) modifies the federal rule by adding the phrase "or statements made by an accused, and pretrial identifications of an accused." This addition is made to emphasize the fact that hearings on the admissibility of all statements made by a criminal defendant, whether inculpatory or exculpatory, must be made outside the presence of the jury. State v. Primus, 312 S.C. 256, 440 S.E.2d 128 (1994); State v. Lee, 255 S.C. 309, 178 S.E.2d 652 (1971). The addition also requires all hearings regarding the admissibility of pretrial identifications (to include any assertion that an in-court identification should be excluded as a result of a pretrial identification) to be heard outside the presence of the jury. State v. Simmons, 308 S.C. 80, 417 S.E.2d 92 (1992).

17

No South Carolina cases have been found which address the matters stated in subsections (d) and (e).

Case Law

"Rule 104(c) unambiguously mandates hearings on the admissibility of out of court identifications of the accused shall in all cases be held outside the presence of the jury. The adoption of Rule 104 did not abrogate the viability of the rulings in the pre-Rules of Evidence cases. The *in camera* hearing required by Rule 104(c) allows a defendant to question a witness more stringently regarding possible misidentification or bias outside the presence of the jury. If the defendant is required to question a victim/witness regarding photographic identification only in the jury's presence, the defendant may be required to severely curtail the questioning so as not to inflame the jury. The trial court erred by denying Cheatham an *in camera* hearing on the admissibility of the identification from the photographic lineup."
State v. Cheatham, 349 S.C. 101, 117, 561 S.E.2d 618, 627 (Ct. App. 2002)

RULE 105
LIMITED ADMISSIBILITY

When evidence which is admissible as to one party or for one purpose but not admissible as to another party or for another purpose is admitted, the court, upon request, shall restrict the evidence to its proper scope and instruct the jury accordingly.

Note:

This rule is identical to the federal rule and is in accord with prior South Carolina law. State v. Bottoms, 260 S.C. 187, 195 S.E.2d 116 (1973); State v. Bagwell, 201 S.C. 387, 23 S.E.2d 244 (1942).

RULE 106
REMAINDER OF OR RELATED WRITINGS OR
STATEMENTS

When a writing, or recorded statement, or part thereof is introduced by a party, an adverse party may require the introduction at that time of any other part or any other writing or recorded statement which ought in fairness to be considered contemporaneously with it.

Note:

The law in this State has been that, when a part of a document or writing is introduced into evidence, the remainder may be introduced by the other party. Dukes v. Smoak, 181 S.C. 182, 186 S.E. 780 (1936). The same rule was applicable to conversations. State v. Jackson, 265 S.C. 278, 217 S.E.2d 794 (1975). However, the party seeking to bring out the remainder had to wait until cross-examination or the presentation of that party's case to do so. This rule, which is identical to the federal rule, changes the prior law as to written or recorded statements. The party seeking to introduce the remainder of a written or recorded statement can now require the remainder to be introduced at the same time the other part of the written or recorded statement is introduced. This rule does not change the order of proof as to the remainder of an unrecorded conversation; the party seeking to bring out the remainder must do so during cross-examination or during that party's case.

Explanation

This is called the rule of completeness. It is about fairness. If one party introduces only a partial piece of evidence, then the judge should require that the party introduce the entire piece of evidence to complete the whole picture.

Case Law

Written/Recorded Statement

"Rule 106 [of the Federal Rules of Evidence] is a procedural device governing the timing of completion evidence; the Rule is 'primarily designed to affect the order of proof'. It means that the adverse party need not wait until cross-examination or rebuttal. As such, the Rule reduces the risk that a writing or recording will be taken out of context and that an initial misleading impression will take hold in the mind of the jury." State v. Cabrera-Pena, 361 S.C. 372, 379 (2004)

Oral/Unrecorded Statement

"The Historical Notes to Rule 106 recognize, however, that adoption of the 'rule does not change the order of proof as to the remainder of an **unrecorded conversation;** the party seeking to bring out the remainder must do so during cross-examination or during that party's case.' Accordingly, Rule 106 merely requires that an oral or unrecorded conversation be brought out upon cross-examination, rather than on direct examination; the rule does not, however, prohibit introduction of oral statements or otherwise vitiate the rule of completeness as it applies to such statements." State v. Cabrera-Pena, 361 S.C. 372, 379–80 (2004)

"We find the common law of this state extends the rule of completeness to oral communications. *Jackson, supra. Accord State v. Eugenio,* 219 Wis.2d 391, 579 N.W.2d 642 (1998) (notwithstanding provision identical to Rule 106 referring only to written or recorded statements, common law rule of completeness continues to exist for oral statements); *State v. Cruz–Meza,* 76 P.3d 1165 (Utah 2003) (recognizing rule of completeness may be applied to oral statements through Rule 611);[3] *State v. Johnson,* 479 A.2d 1284 (Maine 1984). *See also United States v. Haddad,* 10 F.3d 1252 (7th Cir.1993) (citing 1 Weinstein & Berger, *Weinstein's Evidence,* § 106–4 (1992)). Accordingly, where, as here, the state elects to use a witness to elicit portions of a conversation (and incriminating statements therein) made by a defendant, the rule of completeness requires the defendant be permitted to inquire into the full substance of that conversation."

State v. Cabrera-Pena, 361 S.C. 372, 380, 605 S.E.2d 522, 526 (2004)

Article II. Judicial Notice

RULE 201
JUDICIAL NOTICE OF ADJUDICATIVE FACTS

(a) Scope of Rule. This rule governs only judicial notice of adjudicative facts.

(b) Kinds of Facts. A judicially noticed fact must be one not subject to reasonable dispute in that it is either (1) generally known within the territorial jurisdiction of the trial court or (2) capable of accurate and ready determination by resort to sources whose accuracy cannot reasonably be questioned.

(c) When Discretionary. A court may take judicial notice, whether requested or not.

(d) When Mandatory. A court shall take judicial notice if requested by a party and supplied with the necessary information.

(e) Opportunity to Be Heard. A party is entitled upon timely request to an opportunity to be heard as to the propriety of taking judicial notice and the tenor of the matter noticed. In the absence of prior notification, the request may be made after judicial notice has been taken.

(f) Time of Taking Notice. Judicial notice may be taken at any stage of the proceeding.

(g) Instructing Jury. The court shall instruct the jury to accept as conclusive any fact judicially noticed.

Note:

Except for subsection (g), this rule is identical to the federal rule. As stated by subsection (a), this rule governs only judicial notice of adjudicative facts. Adjudicative facts are "facts about the particular event which gave rise to the lawsuit and ... [help] explain who did what, when, where, how and with what motive and intent." Legislative facts, on the other hand, are the factual grounds on which judges base their opinions "when deciding upon the constitutional validity of a statute, interpreting a statute, or extending or restricting a common law rule." C. McCormick, <u>McCormick on Evidence</u> 328 and 331 (4th ed. 1992). The courts of this State continue to have authority to take judicial notice of legislative facts. Cf. <u>Davenport v. City of Rock Hill</u>, 315 S.C. 114, 432 S.E.2d 451 (1993) (history of tax anticipation notes considered).

Subsection (b) is consistent with prior case law in this State. <u>See</u> <u>In Re Harry C.</u>, 280 S.C. 308, 313 S.E.2d 287 (1984); <u>State v. Broad River Power Co.</u>, 177 S.C. 240, 181 S.E. 41 (1935). This rule does not allow a judge to take judicial notice of a fact merely because it is within his personal knowledge, and the case of <u>Gamble v. Price</u>, 289 S.C. 538, 347 S.E.2d 131 (Ct. App.1986) is inconsistent with this rule.

Regarding subsection (c), no South Carolina case has been found discussing this matter.

Subsection (d) is consistent with prior case law in this State. <u>See</u> <u>Toole v. Salter</u>, 249 S.C. 354, 154 S.E.2d 434 (1967); <u>State v. Broad River Power Co.</u>, 177 S.C. 240, 181 S.E. 41 (1935).

Regarding subsection (e), the law of this State has not previously entitled a party to be heard on the issue of taking judicial notice. This opportunity appears to be a useful safeguard to protect a party's rights. J. Weinstein and M. Berger, Weinstein's Evidence, 201[05] (1994).

Subsection (f) is consistent with prior case law in this State. Cf . State v. Squires, 311 S.C. 11, 426 S.E.2d 738 (1992) (Supreme Court took judicial notice that infrared spectroscopy process had gained general acceptance in the scientific community); McCoy v. Town of York, 193 S.C. 390, 8 S.E.2d 905 (1940) (Supreme Court took judicial notice of dangerous qualities of gasoline and kerosene).

Subsection (g) requires a court to instruct the jury to accept as conclusive any fact judicially noticed. The rule differs from the federal rule in that it makes no distinction between civil and criminal cases. The language of the rule is taken from the 1974 Uniform Rules of Evidence, Rule 201.

Case Law

"The State correctly points out that 'Courts will take judicial notice of subjects and facts of general knowledge, and also of facts in the field of any particular science which are capable of demonstration by resort to readily accessible sources of indisputable accuracy, and judges may inform themselves as to such facts by reference to standard works on the subject.' *In re Harry C.,* 280 S.C. 308, 309–10, 313 S.E.2d 287, 288 (1984) (quoting *State v. Newton,* 21 N.C.App. 384, 204 S.E.2d 724, 725 (1974)). But the State overlooks the mandatory nature of a judicially noticed fact under our version of Rule 201 juxtaposed to the constitutionally imposed burden that the State prove each element of the offense.

In all criminal prosecutions, '[t]he government must prove beyond a reasonable doubt every element of a charged offense.' *Victor v. Nebraska,* 511 U.S. 1, 5, 114 S.Ct. 1239, 127 L.Ed.2d 583 (1994) (citing *In re Winship,* 397 U.S. 358, 364, 90 S.Ct. 1068, 25 L.Ed.2d 368 (1970)); *see Dervin v. State,* 386 S.C. 164, 168, 687 S.E.2d 712, 713 (2009) ('Due process requires the State to prove every element of a criminal offense beyond a reasonable doubt.' (citing *State v. Brown,* 360 S.C. 581, 595, 602 S.E.2d 392, 400 (2004))). Here, the jury was instructed to accept as conclusively determined that Appellant was born on June 22, 1973, which established Appellant as eighteen years or older at the time of the offense. The taking of judicial notice of Appellant's date of birth was tantamount to a directed verdict on the element of the accused's age, a practice which is clearly forbidden. *See United Bhd. of Carpenters & Joiners of Am. v. United States,* 330 U.S. 395, 408, 67 S.Ct. 775, 91 L.Ed. 973 (1947) ('[A] judge may not direct a verdict of guilty no matter how conclusive the evidence.')."

State v. Odom, 412 S.C. 253, 267, 772 S.E.2d 149, 155–56 (2015)

" 'A trial court may take judicial notice of a fact only if sufficient notoriety attaches to the fact involved as to make it proper to assume its existence without proof.' *Bowers v. Bowers,* 349 S.C. 85, 94, 561 S.E.2d 610, 615 (Ct.App.2002) (quoting *Eadie v. H.A. Sack Co.,* 322 S.C. 164, 171–72, 470 S.E.2d 397, 401 (Ct.App.1996)). 'A fact is not subject to judicial notice unless the fact is either of such common knowledge that it is accepted by the general public without qualification or contention, or its accuracy may be ascertained by reference to readily available sources of indisputable reliability.' *Id.* (quoting *Eadie,* 322 S.C. at 172, 470 S.E.2d at 401)."

Martin v. Bay, 400 S.C. 140, 152, 732 S.E.2d 667, 674 (Ct. App. 2012)

Article III. Presumptions in Civil Actions and Proceedings

RULE 301
PRESUMPTIONS IN GENERAL IN CIVIL ACTIONS AND PROCEEDINGS

In all civil actions and proceedings not otherwise provided for by statute or by these rules, a presumption imposes on the party against whom it is directed the burden of going forward with evidence to rebut or meet the presumption, but does not shift to such party the burden of proof in the sense of the risk of nonpersuasion, which remains throughout the trial upon the party on whom it was originally cast.

Note:

This rule is the same as the federal rule. It is consistent with the case law in this State. See Long v. Metropolitan Life Insurance Co., 228 S.C. 498, 90 S.E.2d 915 (1956); Ford v. Atlantic Coast Line R. Co., 169 S.C. 41, 168 S.E. 143 (1932).

Case Law

Criminal cases

"This constitutional principle 'prohibits the State from using evidentiary presumptions in a jury charge that have the effect of relieving the State of its burden of persuasion beyond a reasonable doubt of every essential element of a crime.' *Francis v. Franklin,* 471 U.S. 307, 313, 105 S.Ct. 1965, 1970, 85 L.Ed.2d 344 (1985); *Sandstrom v.*

Montana, 442 U.S. 510, 99 S.Ct. 2450, 61 L.Ed.2d 39 (1979). Thus, we have held that mandatory presumptions violate the Due Process Clause if they relieve the State of the burden of persuasion on an element of the offense."
Estelle v. McGuire, 502 U.S. 62, 78, 112 S. Ct. 475, 485, 116 L. Ed. 2d 385 (1991)

Article IV. Relevancy and Its Limits

RULE 401
DEFINITION OF "RELEVANT EVIDENCE"

"Relevant evidence" means evidence having any tendency to make the existence of any fact that is of consequence to the determination of the action more probable or less probable than it would be without the evidence.

Note:

This rule is identical to the federal rule and is consistent with South Carolina law. State v. Alexander, 303 S.C. 377, 401 S.E.2d 146 (1991); State v. Schmidt, 288 S.C. 301, 342 S.E.2d 401 (1986).

Explanation

This rule defines what relevant evidence is. Relevant evidence means that this piece of evidence makes some fact more probable than not. If the judge finds that the piece of evidence is relevant, then they should go to the next rules to determine if they should allow it into evidence. If it is not relevant, then the judge does not let it in.

Case Law

"Evidence is relevant if it tends to establish or to make more or less probable some matter in issue upon which it directly or indirectly bears. Evidence which assists a jury at arriving at

the truth of an issue is relevant and admissible unless otherwise incompetent."
State v. Schmidt, 288 S.C. 301, 303 (1986) (citations omitted)

"In *Francis v. Mauldin*, we held all that is required to render evidence admissible is that the facts shown legally tend to establish, or to make more or less probable, some matter in issue, and to bear directly or indirectly thereon. Relevancy of evidence means the logical relation between the proposed evidence and a fact to be established."
Winburn v. Minnesota Mut. Life Ins. Co., 261 S.C. 568, 574 (1973) (citations omitted)

"Only evidence found to be relevant should be admitted. *Hamilton,* 344 at 353, 543 S.E.2d at 591. 'Under Rule 401, evidence is relevant if it has a direct bearing upon and tends to establish or make more or less probable the matter in controversy.' 'Evidence which assists a jury at arriving at the truth of an issue is relevant and admissible unless otherwise incompetent.' Evidence is incompetent if it could create dangers such as prejudice, undue delay, confusion of the issues, tendency to mislead the jury, waste of time, or cumulative presentation."
State v. Lyles, 379 S.C. 328, 337, 665 S.E.2d 201, 206 (Ct. App. 2008) (citations omitted)

"Evidence is relevant if it tends to make more or less probable a fact in issue. *State v. McWee, supra.* The relevancy of evidence is an issue within the trial judge's discretion."
State v. Huggins, 336 S.C. 200, 205, 519 S.E.2d 574, 576 (1999)

"Evidence is relevant if it tends to make the existence of any fact at issue more or less probable."
State v. Cutro, 365 S.C. 366, 377, 618 S.E.2d 890, 896 (2005)

RULE 402.

RELEVANT EVIDENCE GENERALLY ADMISSIBLE;
IRRELEVANT EVIDENCE INADMISSIBLE

All relevant evidence is admissible, except as otherwise provided by the Constitution of the United States, the Constitution of the State of South Carolina, statutes, these rules, or by other rules promulgated by the Supreme Court of South Carolina. Evidence which is not relevant is not admissible.

Note:

This rule is the federal rule amended to reference South Carolina law. The rule reflects the law in South Carolina. Levy v. Outdoor Resorts of South Carolina, 304 S.C. 427, 405 S.E.2d 387 (1991); State v. Petit, 144 S.C. 452, 142 S.E. 725 (1928).

Case Law

"Evidence is relevant if it tends to establish or to make more or less probable some matter in issue upon which it directly or indirectly bears. Evidence which assists a jury at arriving at the truth of an issue is relevant and admissible unless otherwise incompetent."
State v. Schmidt, 288 S.C. 301, 303 (1986) (citations omitted)

"In *Francis v. Mauldin*, we held all that is required to render evidence admissible is that the facts shown legally tend to establish, or to make more or less probable, some matter in issue, and to bear directly or indirectly thereon. Relevancy of

evidence means the logical relation between the proposed evidence and a fact to be established."
Winburn v. Minnesota Mut. Life Ins. Co., 261 S.C. 568, 574 (1973) (citations omitted)

RULE 403

EXCLUSION OF RELEVANT EVIDENCE ON GROUNDS OF PREJUDICE, CONFUSION, OR WASTE OF TIME

Although relevant, evidence may be excluded if its probative value is substantially outweighed by the danger of unfair prejudice, confusion of the issues, or misleading the jury, or by considerations of undue delay, waste of time, or needless presentation of cumulative evidence.

Note:

This rule is identical to the federal rule and is consistent with the law in South Carolina. State v. Alexander, 303 S.C. 377, 401 S.E.2d 146 (1991) (relevant evidence may be excluded where its probative value is substantially outweighed by the danger of unfair prejudice); State v. Hess, 279 S.C. 14, 301 S.E.2d 547 (limitation of defense testimony upheld where it was merely cumulative to other testimony), cert. denied, 464 U.S. 827, 104 S.Ct. 100, 78 L.Ed.2d 105 (1983); State v. Gregory, 198 S.C. 98, 16 S.E.2d 532 (1941) (trial judge properly limited the defendant's presentation of certain evidence to guard against confusion of the jury by the injection of collateral issues).

Explanation

Even if the evidence is relevant, it should be excluded if it is much more prejudicial or it would just confuse the jury. This is a balancing test. The judge needs to weigh how useful the evidence is versus how prejudicial it is.

Case Law

" 'Probative' means '[t]ending to prove or disprove.' 'Probative value' is the measure of the importance of that tendency to the outcome of a case. It is the weight that a piece of relevant evidence will carry in helping the trier of fact decide the issues. '[T]he more essential the evidence, the greater its probative value.' Thus, a court analyzing probative value considers the importance of the evidence and the significance of the issues to which the evidence relates. As our supreme court stated in *State v. Torres*, '[p]hotographs calculated to arouse the sympathy or prejudice of the jury should be excluded if they are ... not *necessary* to substantiate *material* facts or conditions.' The evaluation of probative value cannot be made in the abstract, but should be made in the practical context of the issues at stake in the trial of each case."
State v. Gray, 408 S.C. 601, 609–10 (Ct. App. 2014)

"As noted in the comment to the Federal Rule, '[u]nfair prejudice' within its context means an undue tendency to suggest decision on an improper basis, commonly, though not necessarily, an emotional one.' "
State v. Alexander, 303 S.C. 377, 382 (1991) (citations omitted)

" 'Unfair prejudice means an undue tendency to suggest a decision on an improper basis.' *State v. Owens,* 346 S.C. 637, 666, 552 S.E.2d 745, 760 (2001) *overruled on other grounds by State v. Gentry,* 363 S.C. 93, 610 S.E.2d 494 (2005). 'An appellate court reviews Rule 403 rulings pursuant to an abuse of discretion standard and gives great deference to the trial court.' *Lee v. Bunch,* 373 S.C. 654, 658, 647 S.E.2d 197, 199 (2007). 'A trial judge's decision regarding the comparative probative value and prejudicial effect of evidence should be reversed only in exceptional circumstances.' "

Johnson v. Horry Cty. Solid Waste Auth., 389 S.C. 528, 534, 698 S.E.2d 835, 838 (Ct. App. 2010)

403 and 404

" 'Once bad act evidence is found admissible under Rule 404(b), the trial court *must* then conduct the prejudice analysis required by Rule 403, SCRE.' *State v. Wallace,* 384 S.C. 428, 435, 683 S.E.2d 275, 278 (2009) (emphasis added). The court may exclude the 404(b) evidence if the probative value of the evidence is substantially outweighed by the danger of unfair prejudice to the defendant. *Id.*
This court has held if 'an on-the-record Rule 403 analysis is required, [we] will not reverse the conviction if the trial judge's comments concerning the matter indicate he was cognizant of the evidentiary rule when admitting the evidence of [a defendant's] prior bad acts.' *State v. King,* 349 S.C. 142, 156, 561 S.E.2d 640, 647 (Ct.App.2002). In *King,* this court determined the trial court's ruling was 'a compressed Rule 403/404(b) analysis' with 'some indicia of his consideration of whether admission of the testimony was fair to King (*i.e.,* more probative than prejudicial).' *Id.* at 157, 561 S.E.2d at 647."
State v. Spears, 403 S.C. 247, 253, 742 S.E.2d 878, 881 (Ct. App. 2013)

RULE 404
CHARACTER EVIDENCE NOT ADMISSIBLE TO PROVE
CONDUCT; EXCEPTION; OTHER CRIMES

(a) Character Evidence Generally. Evidence of a person's character or a trait of character is not admissible for the purpose of proving action in conformity therewith on a particular occasion, except:

> **(1) Character of Accused.** Evidence of a pertinent trait of character offered by an accused, or by the prosecution to rebut the same;

> **(2) Character of Victim.** Evidence of a pertinent trait of character of the victim of the crime offered by an accused, or by the prosecution to rebut the same, or evidence of a character trait of peacefulness of the victim offered by the prosecution in a homicide case to rebut evidence that the victim was the first aggressor;

> **(3) Character of Witness.** Evidence of the character of a witness, as provided in Rules 607, 608, and 609.

(b) Other Crimes, Wrongs, or Acts. Evidence of other crimes, wrongs, or acts is not admissible to prove the character of a person in order to show action in conformity therewith. It may, however, be admissible to show motive, identity, the existence of a common scheme or plan, the absence of mistake or accident, or intent.

Note:

Rule 404(a) is identical to the federal rule and is consistent with the law in South Carolina. State v. Peake, 302 S.C. 378, 396 S.E.2d 362 (1990).

Rule 404(a)(1) is identical to the federal rule and is consistent with the law in South Carolina. State v. Lyles, 210 S.C. 87, 41 S.E.2d 625 (1947) (a defendant may put in evidence of his good character); State v. Major, 301 S.C. 181, 391 S.E.2d 235 (1990) (when the accused offers evidence of his good character regarding specific character traits relevant to the crime charged, the state may cross-examine as to acts relating to the traits focused on by the accused).

Rule 404(a)(2) identical to the federal rule and is consistent with the law in South Carolina. State v. Boyd, 126 S.C. 300, 119 S.E. 839 (1923).

Rule 404(b) differs in two respects from the federal rule. First, unlike the federal rule which does not limit the purposes for which evidence of other crimes may be admitted, the South Carolina rule limits the use of evidence of other crimes, wrongs, or acts to those enumerated in State v. Lyle, 125 S.C. 406, 118 S.E. 803 (1923). See also Citizens Bank of Darlington v. McDonald, 202 S.C. 244, 24 S.E.2d 369 (1943) (Lyle applicable in civil cases). Second, the South Carolina rule does not contain the requirement which is in the federal rule that, upon request by an accused, the prosecution must provide reasonable notice of the general nature of any evidence it intends to introduce under the rule. With the exception of notice of evidence to be used in aggravation in the sentencing phase of capital cases, S.C. Code Ann. § 16-3-20(B) (Supp. 1993), there is no similar requirement under South Carolina law. The rule does not set forth the burden of proof required for the admission of evidence of bad acts not the subject of a conviction and, therefore, case law would

38

control. State v. Smith, 300 S.C. 216, 387 S.E.2d 245 (1989) (in a criminal case, evidence of other crimes or bad acts must be clear and convincing if the acts are not the subject of a conviction). Further, when the prejudicial effect of evidence substantially outweighs its probative value, the evidence may be excluded under Rule 403 which is consistent with prior case law. State v. Garner, 304 S.C. 220, 403 S.E.2d 631 (1991).

Explanation

The general rule: just because someone did something bad in their past, doesn't mean you can use that evidence of that to prove they did something bad now.

However, there are some exceptions:

- ❖ The defendant can put up evidence of his own good character. But if he does this, then the prosecutor can probably bring up bad acts the defendant has done.

- ❖ The defendant can put up evidence of the victim (if it is relevant). If he does this, then the prosecution can bring up their own evidence of the victim.

- ❖ The prosecution/plaintiff cannot bring up bad things the defendant did in his past, just to prove he's doing it again, unless it is evidence to show motive, identity, a common scheme, absence of mistake or accident, or intent. Need to conduct 403 ruling if 404(b) is granted.

Remember, character evidence is substantive evidence that can be used to prove something is true. This is different than impeachment evidence, which is used to discredit a witness's credibility.

Also remember, generally character evidence (404(a)) is not permitted in civil cases unless character is an issue. Prior bad acts evidence (404(b)) can be used in civil cases, but this is usually rare unless it is an intentional tort.

Case Law

Prior bad acts and 403

"Once bad act evidence is found admissible under Rule 404(b), the trial court must then conduct the prejudice analysis required by Rule 403. The probative value of evidence falling within one of the Rule 404(b) exceptions must substantially outweigh the danger of unfair prejudice to the defendant." State v. Wallace, 384 S.C. 428, 435 (2009)

"To admit evidence of prior bad acts, the trial court must first determine whether the proffered evidence is relevant. If the trial court finds the evidence relevant, the court must then determine whether the bad act evidence is admissible under Rule 404(b) to show, *inter alia*, the existence of a common scheme or plan. Even if the testimony is relevant and admissible under Rule 404(b), the trial court must apply Rule 403 and exclude the evidence if its probative value is substantially outweighed by the danger of unfair prejudice to the defendant." State v. Perry, 420 S.C. 643, 654 (Ct. App. 2017) (citations omitted)

"If the defendant was not convicted of the prior crime, evidence of the prior bad act must be clear and convincing." State v. Perry, 420 S.C. 643, 655 (Ct. App. 2017)

Common scheme or plan

"When determining whether evidence is admissible as [part of a] common scheme or plan, the trial court must analyze the similarities and dissimilarities between the crime charged and the bad act evidence to determine whether there is a close degree of similarity."

State v. Perry, 420 S.C. 643, 656 (Ct. App. 2017) (citation omitted)

Motive and intent

"At the conclusion of Robin's *in camera* testimony, the trial judge ruled the October incident was admissible under both the motive and intent exceptions of Rule 404(b) and *Lyle.* In reaching her decision to admit evidence of the October incident, the trial judge stated:

> But I do perceive that it is logically relevant and that ... the State is entitled to give a full snapshot of what happened.
>
> I do not think you can isolate out—this is the incident that started the continuum and does show his intent in going there that evening and his motive in going there that evening.
>
> Which is ... according to the State's theory .... that she was his property and that he was going there to get his property....

We agree that both motive and intent can be inferred from the prior bad act. Following the October assault, Robin reported Sweat's conduct and Sweat spent forty-five days in jail. He was released eleven days before the December incident occurred. Robin became involved with Blake and refused to resume her relationship with Sweat. Within days, Sweat perpetrated the December 11 attack. Thus, the October incident and Sweat's time in jail relate to his actions on December 11, 2001."

State v. Sweat, 362 S.C. 117, 124, 606 S.E.2d 508, 512 (Ct. App. 2004)

Identity

"The trial court and the Court of Appeals found Lambert's testimony admissible under Rule 404(b), SCRE, as evidence of identity. The Court of Appeals asserted the 'testimony was logically relevant as evidence of [Petitioner's] identity because it connected the murder with [Petitioner's] flight from the police one year later.' *Pagan,* 357 S.C. at 144, 591 S.E.2d at 652.

The trial court erred in admitting the bad act evidence because the bad act did not logically relate to the murder. Petitioner's alleged statement to Lambert was that he fled because a female, named Monique or Monica, had accused him of murdering someone and he was out on bond for that murder charge. The failure to stop and the following explanation in no way identifies Petitioner as the person who murdered the victim. This evidence merely illustrates that Petitioner, who had already been charged with the victim's murder and released on bond for that charge, knew he had been accused of murder and knew the name of a witness in the case. *Compare Braxton,* 343 S.C. at 634, 541 S.E.2d at 836 (testimony that witness knew appellant possessed a nine millimeter pistol was relevant because it tended to identify appellant as the possessor of the murder weapon, a nine millimeter pistol); *State v. Cheeseboro,* 346 S.C. 526, 547, 552 S.E.2d 300, 311 (2001) (prior murder was admissible to establish appellant's identity in the prosecution of the current murder where the same weapon was used in both murders)."
State v. Pagan, 369 S.C. 201, 211–12, 631 S.E.2d 262, 267 (2006)

Res gestae

"The *res gestae* theory recognizes evidence of other bad acts may be an integral part of the crime with which the defendant is charged, or may be needed to aid the fact finder in

42

understanding the context in which the crime occurred. This evidence of other crimes is admissible:

when such evidence 'furnishes part of the context of the crime' or is necessary to a 'full presentation' of the case, or is so intimately connected with and explanatory of the crime charged against the defendant and is so much a part of the setting of the case and its 'environment' that its proof is appropriate in order 'to complete the story of the crime on trial by proving its immediate context or the res gestae' or the 'uncharged offense is so linked together in point of time and circumstances with the crime charged that one cannot be fully shown without proving the other ... [and is thus] part of the res gestae of the crime charged.' And where evidence is admissible to provide this 'full presentation of the offense, [t]here is no reason to fragmentize the event under inquiry" by suppressing parts of the res gestae.'"

State v. King, 334 S.C. 504, 512–13 (1999) (citations omitted)

Civil cases

"In 20 Am.Jur., 281, paragraph 303, we find the following discussion: 'There are limitations upon the general rule excluding evidence regarding collateral facts, acts, and conduct. Proof of the existence of other facts, the occurrence of other events, and acts or conduct upon other occasions which have a relevant and material bearing upon a fact in issue before the Court are always admissible in evidence, except as its admissibility may be affected by some of the exclusionary rules of evidence. The law in civil cases, as well as in criminal cases, permits proof of acts other than the one charged which are so related in character, time, and place of commission as to tend to support the conclusion that they were part of a plan or system or as to tend to show the existence of such a plan or system. Where several forgeries were a part of the same transaction and tend to show a common plan or scheme, evidence of other forgeries or alterations is admissible upon an issue of forgery or alteration in a civil case. Where fraud is an issue, evidence of other similar frauds perpetrated by the same person on or about the same time, is admissible particularly where the acts are all part of one general scheme or plan to defraud.' "

Citizens Bank of Darlington v. McDonald, 202 S.C. 244 (1943)

RULE 405
METHODS OF PROVING CHARACTER

(a) Reputation or Opinion. In all cases in which evidence of character or a trait of character of a person is admissible, proof may be made by testimony as to reputation or by testimony in the form of an opinion. On cross-examination, inquiry is allowable into relevant specific instances of conduct.

(b) Specific Instances of Conduct. In cases in which character or a trait of character of a person is an essential element of a charge, claim, or defense, proof may also be made of specific instances of that person's conduct.

Note:

Rule 405(a) is identical to the federal rule and changes the law in South Carolina in one respect. Formerly, only testimony as to a person's general reputation was allowed. State v. Groome, 274 S.C. 189, 262 S.E.2d 31 (1980); In re Greenfield's Estate, 245 S.C. 595, 141 S.E.2d 916 (1965). Rule 405(a) allows evidence of character to be in the form of opinion or reputation evidence. The portion of Rule 405(a) regarding cross-examination as to specific acts is consistent with the law in South Carolina. State v. Major, 301 S.C. 181, 391 S.E.2d 235 (1990) (when the accused offers evidence of his good character regarding specific character traits relevant to the crime charged, the state may cross-examine as to particular bad acts or conduct relating to the traits focused on by the accused).

Rule 405(b) is identical to the federal rule and is consistent with South Carolina law. State v. Amburgey, 206 S.C. 426, 34 S.E.2d 779 (1945).

Explanation

So if you decide that you are going to let in evidence of someone's character, what kind of evidence can they actually put up?

Remember, Rule 404 is divided into two parts: character evidence and other bad acts. Make the party specify what part of the rule they are using. If they want to use 404(A), then continue here. If they want to use prior bad acts 404(B), then go back up a chapter.

A witness can testify about the defendant's/victim's reputation but not specific things he has done. (You only get into specific things when the crime/claim/defense has something to do with character, which is often rare).

Once the door is opened about a person's general reputation, then on cross examination, the other party can ask about relevant specific conduct. This cross examination allows the other party to test the witness's actual knowledge of the person they are vouching for.

Case Law

The following is an example of general reputation of the defendant that the defense put up. Make a note, at this point the defendant has opened the door. So the prosecution would be allowed to ask him or his witness about specific conduct.

"At trial, Harrison testified as to his community involvement, including counseling adolescents. Additionally, Harrison presented the testimony of a character witness, Minnie Cutler, a foster care supervisor with the Berkeley County Department of Social Services and a pastor of a local church. Cutler testified, in essence, as to Harrison's good character and good reputation. Cutler detailed Harrison's volunteer activities at the church. She stated that during the one and one-half years Harrison had been a member of the church, he served as a trusted member of the finance committee and helped renovate the child care center. Cutler described how Harrison 'opened up his home' to two single mothers who needed a place to stay until they could find a job and an apartment."

State v. Harrison, 343 S.C. 165, 170 (Ct. App. 2000)

If character evidence is allowed in, the jury can be instructed that the evidence can be used when deciding guilt or innocence.

"It is well settled that a criminal defendant may introduce evidence of his good character. Furthermore, where requested and there is evidence of good character, a defendant is entitled to an instruction to the effect that evidence of good character and good reputation may in and of itself create a doubt as to guilt and should be considered by the jury, along with all the other evidence, in determining the guilt or innocence of the defendant."

State v. Lee-Grigg, 387 S.C. 310, 317 (2010) (citation omitted)

RULE 406
HABIT; ROUTINE PRACTICE

Evidence of the habit of a person or of the routine practice of an organization, whether corroborated or not and regardless of the presence of eyewitnesses, is relevant to prove that the conduct of the person or organization on a particular occasion was in conformity with the habit or routine practice.

Note:

This rule is identical to the federal rule and makes it clear that the presence or absence of eyewitnesses does not affect the relevancy of evidence of habit or routine practice. To the extent that South Carolina law regarding evidence of habit or routine was previously read to require the absence of eyewitnesses, this rule constitutes a change in the law. Compare Laney v. Atlantic Coast Line Railway Co., 211 S.C. 328, 45 S.E.2d 184 (1947); State v. Hester, 137 S.C. 145, 134 S.E. 885 (1926); Dowling v. Fenner, 131 S.C. 62, 126 S.E. 432 (1922) with Holcombe v. Watson Supply Co., 171 S.C. 110, 171 S.E. 604 (1933).

Case Law

"Federal courts have recognized the tension between Rule 406 (habit) and Rule 404 (character) and noted the difficulty in distinguishing between admissible evidence of habit and inadmissible character evidence.[1] As indicated in the advisory committee's note to Federal Rule of Evidence 406, which is identical to our Rule 406, the distinguishing feature of habit is its degree of specificity. Habit has been described as conduct that is 'situation-specific' or 'specific, particularized conduct capable of almost identical repetition.' *Becker v. ARCO Chem. Co.,* 207 F.3d 176, 204 (3d Cir.2000); *Simplex,* 847 F.2d at 1293. This Court has defined the term 'character,' on the other hand, as 'a generalized description of a person's disposition or a general trait such as honesty, temperance, or peacefulness.' *State v. Nelson,* 331 S.C. at 7, 501 S.E.2d at 718.

State v. Brown, 344 S.C. 70, 74, 543 S.E.2d 552, 554 (2001)

RULE 407
SUBSEQUENT REMEDIAL MEASURES

When, after an event, measures are taken which, if taken previously, would have made the event less likely to occur, evidence of the subsequent measures is not admissible to prove negligence or culpable conduct in connection with the event. This rule does not require the exclusion of evidence of subsequent measures when offered for another purpose, such as proving ownership, control, or feasibility of precautionary measures, if controverted, or impeachment.

Note:

This rule is identical to the federal rule. The general rule that evidence of subsequent measures is inadmissible to establish negligence is consistent with South Carolina law. Green v. Atlantic Coast Line R. Co., 136 S.C. 337, 134 S.E. 385 (1926). Under South Carolina law another stated purpose for admitting evidence of subsequent measures is to show the conditions existing at the time of the event or accident. Taylor v. Nix, 307 S.C. 551, 416 S.E.2d 619 (1992); Plunkett v. Clearwater Bleachery Mfg. Co., 80 S.C. 310, 61 S.E. 431 (1906); see also Eargle v. Sumter Lighting Co., 110 S.C. 560, 96 S.E. 909 (1918).

Case Law

"The rationale underlying Rule 407 'rests on a social policy of encouraging people to take, or at least not discouraging them from taking, steps in furtherance of added safety.' Fed.R.Evid. 407 advisory committee's note.[5] In *Webb v. CSX Transportation, Inc.*, 364 S.C. 639, 653, 615 S.E.2d 440, 448

(2005), this Court reversed and remanded a train collision case, in part, because of the erroneous admission of evidence of post-accident vegetation cutting. The *Webb* court rejected the narrow application of Rule 407 used in *Reiland v. Southland Equipment Service, Inc.*, 330 S.C. 617, 500 S.E.2d 145 (Ct.App.1998), and held, 'Rule 407 bars the introduction of any change, repair, or precaution that under the plaintiff's theory would have made the accident less likely to happen, unless the evidence is offered for another purpose.' *Webb*, 364 S.C. at 653, 615 S.E.2d at 448.

Appellant argues the circuit judge should have recognized the impeachment exception to Rule 407 to admit the evidence of subsequent remedial measures, and additionally argues that CSX waived its right to object to the admission of Exhibit 134. We disagree.

A. Impeachment of CSX's Position that the Sight Distance was Adequate

Appellant contends she should have been permitted to introduce evidence of post-accident cutting to impeach CSX's position that the available sight distance on May 30, 2004, was adequate and that the vegetation did not need to be cut. We disagree. Allowing a party to invoke the impeachment exception to Rule 407 in response to the opposing party's general defense against a negligence claim would swallow the rule. The Supreme Court of Illinois encountered a party propounding this same logic and stated:

> Just as evidence of subsequent remedial measures is not considered sufficiently probative to be admissible to prove prior negligence, that evidence is not admissible for impeachment where the sole value of the impeachment rests on that same impermissible inference of prior negligence."

Carson v. CSX Transp., Inc., 400 S.C. 221, 234–35, 734 S.E.2d 148, 155 (2012)

RULE 408
COMPROMISE AND OFFERS TO COMPROMISE

Evidence of (1) furnishing or offering or promising to furnish, or (2) accepting or offering or promising to accept, a valuable consideration in compromising or attempting to compromise a claim which was disputed as to either validity or amount, is not admissible to prove liability for or invalidity of the claim or its amount. Evidence of conduct or statements made in compromise negotiations is likewise not admissible. This rule does not require the exclusion of any evidence otherwise discoverable merely because it is presented in the course of compromise negotiations. This rule also does not require exclusion when the evidence is offered for another purpose, such as proving bias or prejudice of a witness, negativing a contention of undue delay, or proving an effort to obstruct a criminal investigation or prosecution.

Note:

This rule is identical to the federal rule. It is generally the rule in South Carolina that evidence relating to settlements is not admissible to prove liability. Hunter v. Hyder, 236 S.C. 378, 114 S.E.2d 493 (1960); see also Woodward v. Southern Railway, 88 S.C. 453, 70 S.E. 1060 (1911) (evidence of disclosures made by either party to the other, directly or indirectly, in negotiations for a compromise is not admissible). Evidence of an offer to compromise may be admissible for some other purpose. Meehan v. Commercial Casualty Ins. Co., 166 S.C. 496, 165 S.E. 194 (1932) (evidence of offers of compromise made by alleged agent of a party admissible for purpose of proving agency).

Case Law

"This rule contemplates that the parties need to feel free to make certain assumptions for the purpose of settlement negotiations and that those statements are assumed by the author to be true only for the purpose of compromise negotiations. The rule codifies the longstanding principle that evidence of conduct or statements made in compromise negotiations is not admissible. *See QHG of Lake City, Inc. v. McCutcheon,* 360 S.C. 196, 209, 600 S.E.2d 105, 111 (Ct.App.2004) ('Because the law favors compromises, our appellate courts have long held that testimony as to negotiations and offers to compromise are inadmissible for proving liability.'); *Commerce Ctr. of Greenville, Inc. v. W. Powers McElveen **810 & Assocs., Inc.,* 347 S.C. 545, 558, 556 S.E.2d 718, 725 (Ct.App.2001) ('The courts favor compromise; accordingly, evidence relating to settlements is generally not admissible to prove liability.'); *Hunter v. Hyder,* 236 S.C. 378, 387, 114 S.E.2d 493, 497 (1960) ('[C]ompromises are favored and evidence of an offer or attempt to compromise or settle a matter in dispute cannot be given in evidence against the party by whom such offer or attempt was made.')."

Fesmire v. Digh, 385 S.C. 296, 307–08, 683 S.E.2d 803, 809–10 (Ct. App. 2009)

RULE 409
PAYMENT OF MEDICAL AND SIMILAR EXPENSES

Evidence of furnishing or offering or promising to pay medical, hospital, or similar expenses occasioned by an injury is not admissible to prove liability for the injury.

Note:

This rule is identical to the federal rule. Formerly, South Carolina law, while generally prohibiting the admission of evidence of offers to pay, or payment of, medical or other expenses, <u>McIntire v. Winn Dixie Greenville, Inc.</u>, 275 S.C. 323, 270 S.E.2d 440 (1980), did allow its admission if the circumstances surrounding the payment indicated an admission of liability rather than an act of benevolence. <u>Crosby v. Southeast Zayre, Inc.</u>, 274 S.C. 519, 265 S.E.2d 517 (1980). The rule strictly prohibits the admission of evidence of offers to pay, or payment of, medical or other similar expenses.

RULE 410
INADMISSIBILITY OF PLEAS, PLEA DISCUSSIONS, AND
RELATED STATEMENTS

Except as otherwise provided in this rule, evidence of the following is not, in any civil or criminal proceeding, admissible against the defendant who made the plea or was a participant in the plea discussions:

(1) a plea of guilty which was later withdrawn;

(2) a plea of nolo contendere;

(3) any statement made in the course of any court proceedings regarding either of the foregoing pleas; or

(4) any statement made in the course of plea discussions with an attorney for the prosecuting authority which do not result in a plea of guilty or which result in a plea of guilty later withdrawn.

However, such a statement is admissible (i) in any proceeding wherein another statement made in the course of the same plea or plea discussions has been introduced and the statement ought in fairness be considered contemporaneously with it, or (ii) in a criminal proceeding for perjury or false statement if the statement was made by the defendant under oath, on the record and in the presence of counsel.

Note:

Except for subsection (3), this rule is identical to the federal rule. Subsection (3) was amended because South Carolina has

no equivalent to Rule 11 of the Federal Rules of Criminal Procedure. It should be noted that convictions based on pleas of nolo contendere are admissible under Rule 609 for impeachment. The rule is consistent with prior South Carolina law. State v. Mathis, 287 S.C. 589, 340 S.E.2d 538 (1986); State v. Lynn, 277 S.C. 222, 284 S.E.2d 786 (1981).

Case Law

Defendant may waive this right

"We agree with the Court of Appeals that a criminal defendant may waive the protections afforded by Rule 410. Here, petitioner and his attorney executed an agreement wherein petitioner agreed that if a subsequent polygraph examination demonstrated deception, inconsistencies, or that petitioner shot the victim, then 'the terms of this proffer are null and void **and** any statements made by [petitioner] may be used against him by the State for any legal purpose, including ... disposition of charges through plea or trial ... and impeachment.' Proffer Agreement section 2 (emphasis supplied). Further, section 7 provides in relevant part not only that petitioner's violation of the Agreement would render the Proffer's terms null and void, but also that 'the State shall have the right to use any information obtained through this Proffer in any fashion, whether direct [or] collateral....' Applying the rules of contract construction here, 'regardless of the agreement's wisdom or lack thereof,' we agree with the Court of Appeals that, on this record, petitioner's Proffer Agreement, entered with the advice and consent of counsel, waived the protections of Rule 410, SCRE."
State v. Wills, 409 S.C. 183, 185, 762 S.E.2d 3, 4 (2014)

RULE 411
LIABILITY INSURANCE

Evidence that a person was or was not insured against liability is not admissible upon the issue whether the person acted negligently or otherwise wrongfully. This rule does not require the exclusion of evidence of insurance against liability when offered for another purpose, such as proof of agency, ownership, or control, or bias or prejudice of a witness.

Note:

This rule is identical to the federal rule and is consistent with the law in South Carolina. Dunn v. Charleston Coca-Cola Bottling Co., 311 S.C. 43, 426 S.E.2d 756 (1993) (the fact that a defendant is protected from liability by insurance shall not be made known to the jury); Sarvis v. Register, 288 S.C. 236, 341 S.E.2d 791 (1986) (generally, the existence of insurance should not be brought to the attention of the jury).

Explanation

It is improper for a party to bring up liability insurance for the purpose of showing negligence. However, it may be used for a different purpose, such as bias or ownership. If a judge finds that 411 does not apply (e.g., liability is admitted), then the judge would still need to have a 403 ruling to decide if the evidence of insurance should be admitted.

Case Law

Liability admitted

57

"In *Yoho,* we adopted a framework for analysis in considering whether or not to admit evidence of insurance. We held that if Rule 411 does not require the exclusion of evidence of insurance, the court should then proceed to perform Rule 403 analysis and consider whether the probative value of the evidence is substantially outweighed by the prejudicial effect and potential for confusing the jury. *Yoho,* 345 S.C. at 365, 548 S.E.2d at 586. As liability was admitted in this case, Rule 411 is not implicated and the question whether the records are admissible turns on Rule 403."
Todd v. Joyner, 385 S.C. 421, 424, 685 S.E.2d 595, 596–97 (2009)

Expert witness for insurance company

"Rule 411, SCRE (emphasis added). As Thompson admitted liability, the unquestioned purpose of the requested cross-examination was to prove bias, and not liability. Moreover, the evidence Yoho sought to introduce was relevant to the issue of Dr. Brannon's bias."
Yoho v. Thompson, 345 S.C. 361, 365, 548 S.E.2d 584, 586 (2001)

"We adopt the substantial connection analysis and conclude the connection between Dr. Brannon and Nationwide was sufficient to justify admitting evidence of their relationship to demonstrate Dr. Brannon's possible bias in favor of Nationwide. Dr. Brannon was not merely being paid an expert's fee in this matter. Instead, he maintained an employment relationship with Nationwide and other insurance companies. Dr. Brannon consulted for Nationwide in other cases and gave lectures to Nationwide's agents and adjusters. Ten to twenty percent of Dr. Brannon's practice consisted of reviewing records for insurance companies,

including Nationwide. Further, Dr. Brannon's yearly salary was based in part on his insurance consulting work. The trial court erred in refusing to allow Yoho to cross-examine Dr. Brannon about his relationship with Nationwide."
Yoho v. Thompson, 345 S.C. 361, 366, 548 S.E.2d 584, 586 (2001)

RULE 412

ADMISSIBILITY OF EVIDENCE CONCERNING VICTIM'S SEXUAL CONDUCT IN CRIMINAL SEXUAL CONDUCT CASES

In prosecutions for criminal sexual conduct or assault with intent to commit criminal sexual conduct, the admissibility of evidence concerning the victim's sexual conduct is subject to the limitations contained in S.C. Code Ann. 16-3-659.1 (1985).

Note:

In a prosecution for criminal sexual conduct or assault with intent to commit criminal sexual conduct, the admissibility of evidence of the victim's sexual conduct is controlled by S.C. Code Ann. 16-3-659.1 (1985). Unlike the federal rule which contains the standards and procedures governing the admissibility of such evidence, this rule merely references the statute.

Case Law

"Because Grovenstein's trial commenced on January 16, 1996, the new Rules of Evidence were in effect. We note, however, the Rape Shield Statute has not been altered by the adoption of these rules. *See* Rule 412, SCRE ('In prosecutions for criminal sexual conduct or assault with intent to commit criminal sexual conduct, the admissibility of evidence concerning the victim's sexual conduct is subject to the limitations contained in S.C.Code Ann. § 16-3-659.1 (1985).')."

State v. Grovenstein, 340 S.C. 210, 215, 530 S.E.2d 406, 409 (Ct. App. 2000)

§ 16-3-659.1. Criminal sexual conduct; admissibility of evidence concerning victim's sexual conduct.

(1) Evidence of specific instances of the victim's sexual conduct, opinion evidence of the victim's sexual conduct, and reputation evidence of the victim's sexual conduct is not admissible in prosecutions under Sections 16-3-615 and 16-3-652 to 16-3-656; however, evidence of the victim's sexual conduct with the defendant or evidence of specific instances of sexual activity with persons other than the defendant introduced to show source or origin of semen, pregnancy, or disease about which evidence has been introduced previously at trial is admissible if the judge finds that such evidence is relevant to a material fact and issue in the case and that its inflammatory or prejudicial nature does not outweigh its probative value. Evidence of specific instances of sexual activity which would constitute adultery and would be admissible under rules of evidence to impeach the credibility of the witness may not be excluded.

(2) If the defendant proposes to offer evidence described in subsection (1), the defendant, prior to presenting his defense shall file a written motion and offer of proof. The court shall order an in-camera hearing to determine whether the proposed evidence is admissible under subsection (1). If new evidence is discovered during the presentation of the defense that may make the evidence described in subsection (1) admissible, the judge may order an in-camera hearing to determine whether the proposed evidence is admissible under subsection (1).
S.C. Code Ann. § 16-3-659.1

Article V. Privileges

RULE 501
GENERAL RULE

Except as required by the Constitution of South Carolina, by the Constitution of the United States or by South Carolina statute, the privilege of a witness, person or government shall be governed by the principles of the common law as they may be interpreted by the courts in the light of reason and experience.

Note:

This rule modifies the federal rule to refer to the South Carolina Constitution and statutes. Like the federal rule, this rule does not set forth a list of privileges. Among those privileges which would be covered by this rule are: husband and wife (S.C. Code Ann. 19-11-30); priest and penitent (S.C. Code Ann. 19-11-90); certain mental health professionals and clients (S.C. Code Ann. 19-11-95); news media and sources (S.C. Code Ann. 19-11-100); attorney and client [Drayton v. Industrial Life & Health Ins. Co., 205 S.C. 98, 31 S.E.2d 148 (1944)]; privilege against self-incrimination (U.S. Const. amend. V; S.C. Const. art. I, 12; S.C. Code Ann. 19-11-80); and the identity of a confidential informant [State v. Hayward, 302 S.C. 75, 393 S.E.2d 918 (1990)].

Case Law

"Thus, unlike many other jurisdictions, South Carolina does not delineate specific privileges through its rules of evidence.

Rather, our evidentiary privileges are provided through an assortment of sources: the South Carolina or United States Constitution, the common law, or a statutory provision.

When construing a purported statutory privilege, there is no requirement that the word 'privilege' be used by the General Assembly in order to evidence an intent to create one. See, e.g., State v. Copeland, 321 S.C. 318, 323, 468 S.E.2d 620, 624 (1996) (citing section 19-11-30 of the South Carolina Code of Laws as providing a marital privilege although the statute does not use the word 'privilege' and simply states 'no husband or wife may be required to disclose any confidential or, in a criminal proceeding, any communication made by one to the other during their marriage' (emphasis added)). Our role as a court, of course, is to interpret a statute to discern and effectuate legislative intent. Charleston Cty. Sch. Dist. v. State Budget & Control Bd., 313 S.C. 1, 5, 437 S.E.2d 6, 8 (1993) ('The cardinal rule of statutory construction is to ascertain and effectuate the intent of the legislature.')."

Hartsock v. Goodyear Dunlop Tires N. Am. Ltd., 422 S.C. 643, 649, 813 S.E.2d 696, 699–700 (2018)

Article VI. Witnesses

RULE 601
COMPETENCY

(a) General Rule. Every person is competent to be a witness except as otherwise provided by statute or these rules.

(b) Disqualification of a Witness. A person is disqualified to be a witness if the court determines that (1) the proposed witness is incapable of expressing himself concerning the matter as to be understood by the judge and jury either directly or through interpretation by one who can understand him, or (2) the proposed witness is incapable of understanding the duty of a witness to tell the truth.

Note:

Subsection (a) differs from the federal rule which provides that the only exceptions to the competency rule are those set forth in the Rules of Evidence. Because legislation such as the Dead Man's Statute, S.C. Code Ann. § 19-11-20 (1985), still exists limiting witness competency, the rule also refers to exceptions provided by statute.

At common law, there were numerous grounds which would render a witness incompetent. Legislation has eliminated many of these common law disqualifications resulting in a liberalization of the rules regarding competency.See, e.g., S.C. Code Ann. §§ 19-11-10 (1985) (party competent to be witness); 19-11-30 (Supp. 1993) (spouse of party competent); 19-11-40 (1985) (witness having interest in action is not disqualified); 19-11-50 (1985) (criminal defendant may testify); 19-11-60 (1985) (convicted person may testify). Subsection (a) continues this trend of liberalization by creating a general rule of competency.

This rule will result in a change in the law regarding competency of children. Under prior South Carolina law, proof of competency for children under the age of fourteen was required unless the child was a victim of abuse or neglect, as defined in the Children's Code, who was testifying concerning the abuse or neglect. South Carolina Department of Social Services v. Doe, 292 S.C. 211, 355 S.E.2d 543 (Ct. App.1987); S.C. Code Ann. § 19-11-25 (Supp. 1993). Under this rule, children are presumed to be competent unless it is shown otherwise.

The federal rule does not contain a subsection (b). This provision was added to establish a minimum standard for competency of a witness and to make it clear that the determination of a witness' competency is within the sound discretion of the trial judge. In re Robert M., 294 S.C. 69, 362 S.E.2d 639 (1987); State v. Camele, 293 S.C. 302, 360 S.E.2d 307 (1987); State v. Pitts, 256 S.C. 420, 182 S.E.2d 738 (1971).

Case Law

" 'Every person is competent to be a witness except as otherwise provided by statute or these rules.' Rule 601(a), SCRE. Courts presume a witness to be competent because bias or other defects in a witness's testimony—revealed primarily through cross examination—affect a witness's credibility and may be weighed by the factfinder. *See State v. Smith,* 199 S.C. 279, 282, 19 S.E.2d 224, 225 (1942) ('the established practice [is] to allow a rather full and thorough cross-examination of the witnesses for both the State and the defendant in the criminal Courts by way of questions tending to test memory, veracity or credibility'); *accord* Mueller and Kirkpatrick, *Modern Evidence,* § 6.1 (1995); 98 C.J.S. *Witnesses* § 458 (1957).

A witness must have personal knowledge of the matter and must swear or affirm to tell the truth. Rules 602 and 603, SCRE. 'A person is disqualified to be a witness if the court determines that ... the proposed witness is incapable of understanding the duty of a witness to tell the truth.' Rule 601(b)(2), SCRE.[2] The purpose of Rule 601(b) is to provide a minimum standard for the competency of a witness. Notes to Rule 601, SCRE. Even a convicted perjurer may testify as long as he or she meets the minimum standard. *See State v. Merriman,* 287 S.C. 74, 337 S.E.2d 218 (Ct.App.1985) (explaining the abolition of the prohibition against testimony by a convicted perjurer)."

State v. Needs, 333 S.C. 134, 142–43, 508 S.E.2d 857, 861 (1998), holding modified by State v. Cherry, 361 S.C. 588, 606 S.E.2d 475 (2004)

"Even in cases involving videotaped depositions, a trial judge should make a judicial determination of competency through his **personal observations** of a witness while that witness is being questioned.[1] In the instant case, the trial court concluded that the videotape was admissible and that the victim was a competent witness solely upon the Assistant Solicitor's assertions. Surely, statements from advocates for either party in a judicial proceeding evaluating a witness' competency cannot substitute for a trial judge's personal observations of a person's capacity to be a competent witness. In our view, the trial judge abused his discretion by failing to view the videotaped deposition before admitting it into evidence. We further conclude that the trial judge erred in making a competency determination[2] based upon the

Assistant Solicitor's representations, rather than upon his personal observations."
State v. Camele, 293 S.C. 302, 304, 360 S.E.2d 307, 308 (1987) (citations omitted)

RULE 602
LACK OF PERSONAL KNOWLEDGE

A witness may not testify to a matter unless evidence is introduced sufficient to support a finding that the witness has personal knowledge of the matter. Evidence to prove personal knowledge may, but need not, consist of the witness' own testimony. This rule is subject to the provisions of Rule 703, relating to opinion testimony by expert witnesses.

Note:

This rule is identical to the federal rule and is consistent with South Carolina law. See Gentry v. Watkins-Carolina Trucking Co., 249 S.C. 316, 154 S.E.2d 112 (1967); Wilson v. Clary, 212 S.C. 250, 47 S.E.2d 618 (1948).

Case Law

"Tennant also sought to use Dr. Schwartz–Watts to introduce his out-of-court assertions that the victim had visited him in jail after having obtained an order of protection against him. These assertions were made to another doctor and recorded in that doctor's notes. Dr. Schwartz–Watts had no personal knowledge of the victim's alleged visits with Tennant, and this factual issue required no special expertise. Thus, the testimony was properly excluded. Rule 602, SCRE (requiring a witness other than an expert to have personal knowledge of the matters testified to); *cf. State v. Douglas,* 380 S.C. 499, 501–03 & n. 2, 671 S.E.2d 606, 608–09 & n. 2 (2009) (holding a forensic interviewer's personal observations of alleged victims did not require

specialized knowledge, and therefore, qualification as an expert was unnecessary)."
State v. Tennant, 394 S.C. 5, 12, 714 S.E.2d 297, 300 (2011)

"The GAL testified she reviewed Mother's medical records with Mother and Mother's attorney; thus, she had personal knowledge of the records."
Saj v. Saj, No. 2015-UP-571, 2015 WL 9393948, at *1 (S.C. Ct. App. Dec. 23, 2015)

"On the other hand, a lay witness may only testify as to matters within his personal knowledge and may not offer opinion testimony which requires special knowledge, skill, experience, or training."
Watson v. Ford Motor Co., 389 S.C. 434, 446, 699 S.E.2d 169, 175 (2010)

"A witness must have personal knowledge of the matter and must swear or affirm to tell the truth. Rules 602 and 603, SCRE."
State v. Needs, 333 S.C. 134, 142, 508 S.E.2d 857, 861 (1998), holding modified by State v. Cherry, 361 S.C. 588, 606 S.E.2d 475 (2004)

RULE 603

OATH OR AFFIRMATION

Before testifying, every witness shall be required to declare that the witness will testify truthfully, by oath or affirmation administered in a form calculated to awaken the witness' conscience and impress the witness' mind with the duty to do so.

Note:

This rule is identical to the federal rule which sets forth the common law tenet that a witness is required to take an oath or affirmation to tell the truth before being allowed to testify. See 98 C.J.S. Witnesses § 320(a) (1957). The use of an affirmation instead of an oath is consistent with prior law. See S.C. Code Ann. § 19-1-40 (1985); Rule 43(d), SCRCP.

Case Law

"A witness must have personal knowledge of the matter and must swear or affirm to tell the truth. Rules 602 and 603, SCRE."
State v. Needs, 333 S.C. 134, 142, 508 S.E.2d 857, 861 (1998), holding modified by State v. Cherry, 361 S.C. 588, 606 S.E.2d 475 (2004)

RULE 604
INTERPRETERS

An interpreter is subject to the provisions of these rules relating to qualification as an expert and the administration of an oath or affirmation to make a true translation.

Note:

This rule is identical to the federal rule. The qualification of an interpreter is within the discretion of the trial judge and depends on the circumstances of each case. Peoples National Bank v. Manos Brothers, 226 S.C. 257, 84 S.E.2d 857 (1954).

Case Law

"Affirmed pursuant to Rule 220(b), SCACR, and the following authorities: *Melton v. Olenik,* 379 S.C. 45, 50–54, 664 S.E.2d 487, 490–93 (Ct.App.2008) (holding the appointment of a qualified interpreter lies within the trial court's discretion); S.C.Code Ann. § 17–1–50(A)(4) (2003) ('Qualified interpreter' means a person who: (a) is eighteen years of age or older; (b) is not a family member of a party or a witness; (c) is not a person confined to an institution; and (d) has education, training, or experience that enables him to speak English and a foreign language fluently, and is readily able to interpret simultaneously and consecutively and to sight-translate documents from English into the language....'); *Peoples Nat. Bank of Greenville v. Manos Bros., Inc.,* 226 S.C. 257, 280, 84 S.E.2d 857, 868 (1954) (overruled on other grounds) ('The qualifications of an interpreter depend much on the circumstances, and should be left for the determination of the trial court.'); Rule 1, RPCCI,

Rule 511, SCACR ('Interpreters shall render a complete and accurate interpretation, or sight translation, without altering, omitting or adding anything to what is stated or written, and without explanation or summarization.'); Rule 3, RPCCI, Rule 511, SCACR ('Interpreters shall be impartial and unbiased and shall refrain from conduct that may give an appearance of bias. Interpreters shall disclose any real or perceived conflict of interest.'); Rule 3, RPCCI, Rule 511, SCACR, cmt. (instructing the existence of a potential conflict of interest 'does not alone disqualify an interpreter from providing services as long as the interpreter is able to render services objectively')."

State v. Deqing Chen, No. 2012-UP-675, 2012 WL 10864565, at *1 (S.C. Ct. App. Dec. 19, 2012)

RULE 605
COMPETENCY OF JUDGE AS WITNESS

The judge presiding at the trial may not testify in that trial as a witness.

Note:

This rule is identical to the first sentence of the federal rule and is consistent with South Carolina law providing that a judge may not testify as a witness in a case being tried before that judge. State v. Bagwell, 201 S.C. 387, 23 S.E.2d 244 (1942). The second sentence of the federal rule dispenses with the requirement of an objection to a judge being a witness. This sentence was deleted as being inconsistent with the law of this state. See State v. Torrence, 305 S.C. 45, 406 S.E.2d 315 (1991).

RULE 606

COMPETENCY OF JUROR AS WITNESS

(a) At the Trial. A member of the jury may not testify as a witness before that jury in the trial of the case in which the juror is sitting. If the juror is called so to testify, the opposing party shall be afforded an opportunity to object outside the presence of the jury.

(b) Inquiry Into Validity of Verdict or Indictment. Upon an inquiry into the validity of a verdict or indictment, a juror may not testify as to any matter or statement occurring during the course of the jury's deliberations or to the effect of anything upon that or any other juror's mind or emotions as influencing the juror to assent to or dissent from the verdict or indictment or concerning the juror's mental processes in connection therewith, except that a juror may testify on the question whether extraneous prejudicial information was improperly brought to the jury's attention or whether any outside influence was improperly brought to bear upon any juror. Nor may a juror's affidavit or evidence of any statement by the juror concerning a matter about which the juror would be precluded from testifying be received for these purposes.

Note:

The language of this rule is identical to the federal rule. Subsection (a) of this rule changes the law in South Carolina in two regards. First, while prior law allowed a juror to testify as to venue, State v. Vari, 35 S.C. 175, 14 S.E. 392 (1892) (juror allowed to testify as to isolated, particular matter such as value or venue but not as to general facts and circumstances of the offense), this subsection would prohibit such testimony. Second, the prior law did not require that the party opposing the calling of a juror as a witness be given an opportunity to object outside the presence of the jury.

Subsection (b) is consistent with the general rule that a juror may not present testimony as to the deliberations in the jury room; as to any mistake, irregularity, or misconduct on the part of the jurors; or which would impeach the verdict or contradict the record. <u>Barsh v. Chrysler Corp.</u>, 262 S.C. 129, 203 S.E.2d 107 (1974); <u>State v. Wells</u>, 249 S.C. 249, 153 S.E.2d 904 (1967); <u>Caines v. Marion Coca-Cola Bottling Co.</u>, 196 S.C. 502, 14 S.E.2d 10 (1941). An affidavit of a juror has been admitted on a post-trial motion "with great hesitation" when there was an allegation that a party had attempted to influence the juror. <u>Cohen v. Robert</u>, 33 S.C.L. (2 Strob.) 410 (1848). The rule is also consistent with South Carolina cases holding that no one may invade the secrecy of a grand jury's deliberations. <u>State v. Sanders</u>, 251 S.C. 431, 163 S.E.2d 220 (1968); <u>Margolis v. Telech</u>, 239 S.C. 232, 122 S.E.2d 417 (1961).

Case Law

"Under Rule 606(b), SCRE, a juror's testimony or affidavit as to what occurred during deliberations is not admissible to challenge 'the validity of the verdict.' However, Rule 606(b) allows the admission of a juror's testimony or affidavit 'on the question whether extraneous prejudicial information was improperly brought to the jury's attention or whether any outside influence was improperly brought to bear upon any juror.' The trial court explained the affidavit did not 'give rise to allegations of external misconduct' because it did not allege the jury received evidence or influence from outside sources.

We find there is evidence to support the trial court's determination that none of the information in the foreperson's affidavit is extraneous or relates to outside influence."
Lynch v. Carolina Self Storage Centers, Inc., 409 S.C. 146, 152, 760 S.E.2d 111, 115 (Ct. App. 2014)

"For a considerable period of history, the rule in South Carolina was that a juror's testimony was not admissible to prove either a juror's own misconduct or the misconduct of fellow jurors. *State v. Thomas,* 268 S.C. 343, 348, 234 S.E.2d 16, 18 (1977) (*citing Barsh v. Chrysler Corp., 262 S.C. 129, 203 S.E.2d 107 (1974)*). Rule 606(b) of the South Carolina Rules of Evidence alters this common law rule by allowing a juror to offer testimony as to 'whether extraneous prejudicial information was improperly brought to the jury's attention or whether any outside influence was improperly brought to bear upon any juror.' ...
Rule 606 thus draws a distinction between evidence of external influences on the jury's deliberations and comments of jurors occurring during deliberations. While the rule allows evidence of the former to be introduced, it prohibits the introduction of the latter.
Although Rule 606 expressly prohibits the introduction of juror testimony regarding both the content and the effect of statements occurring during the jury's deliberations, this Court has recognized an exception to that categorical prohibition. In *State v. Hunter,* this Court held that juror testimony involving internal misconduct may be received only when necessary to ensure fundamental fairness."
Shumpert v. State, 378 S.C. 62, 66–67, 661 S.E.2d 369, 371 (2008)

"As a general rule, juror testimony may not be the basis for impeaching a jury verdict.[1] Normally, courts should not intrude into the privacy of the jury room to scrutinize how

jurors reached their verdict. However, other jurisdictions have made exceptions based on the nature of the alleged misconduct. When an extraneous influence is alleged, juror testimony can normally be used. If the alleged misconduct is internal, courts are more strict.[2] Normally, juror testimony involving internal misconduct is competent only when necessary to ensure due process, i.e. fundamental fairness."
State v. Hunter, 320 S.C. 85, 88, 463 S.E.2d 314, 316 (1995)

"Juror testimony regarding internal misconduct is generally inadmissible to impeach a verdict except when necessary to ensure fundamental fairness. *State v. Hunter,* 320 S.C. 85, 463 S.E.2d 314 (1995); *see also* Rule 606(b), SCRE effective September 3, 1995. Based on our review of the record, we concur in Judge Macaulay's ruling that the proffered evidence was inadmissible."
Ex parte Greenville News, 326 S.C. 1, 3, 482 S.E.2d 556, 557 (1997)

RULE 607
WHO MAY IMPEACH

The credibility of a witness may be attacked by any party, including the party calling the witness.

Note:

This rule is identical to the federal rule. However, it is contrary to the former law in this State that a party must vouch for its own witness and may not impeach its witness unless the witness is declared hostile upon a showing of actual surprise and harm, or unless the party is required to call someone, such as a subscribing witness to a deed or will, as a witness. State v. Anderson, 304 S.C. 551, 406 S.E.2d 152 (1991); Hicks v. Coleman, 240 S.C. 227, 125 S.E.2d 473 (1962); White v. Southern Oil Stores, Inc., 198 S.C. 173, 17 S.E.2d 150 (1941).

Case Law

"Prior to our adoption of Rule 607, SCRE, the party who called a witness was said to vouch for the witness's credibility, and it was improper to impeach one's own witness unless the witness was first declared hostile."
State v. Sierra, 337 S.C. 368, 379, 523 S.E.2d 187, 192–93 (Ct. App. 1999)

RULE 608
EVIDENCE OF CHARACTER, CONDUCT AND BIAS OF
WITNESS

(a) Opinion and Reputation Evidence of Character. The credibility of a witness may be attacked or supported by evidence in the form of opinion or reputation, but subject to these limitations: (1) the evidence may refer only to character for truthfulness or untruthfulness, and (2) evidence of truthful character is admissible only after the character of the witness for truthfulness has been attacked by opinion or reputation evidence or otherwise.

(b) Specific Instances of Conduct. Specific instances of the conduct of a witness, for the purpose of attacking or supporting the witness' credibility, other than conviction of crime as provided in Rule 609, may not be proved by extrinsic evidence. They may, however, in the discretion of the court, if probative of truthfulness or untruthfulness, be inquired into on cross-examination of the witness (1) concerning the witness' character for truthfulness or untruthfulness, or (2) concerning the character for truthfulness or untruthfulness of another witness as to which character the witness being cross-examined has testified.

The giving of testimony, whether by an accused or by any other witness, does not operate as a waiver of the accused's or the witness' privilege against self-incrimination when examined with respect to matters which relate only to credibility.

(c) Evidence of Bias. Bias, prejudice or any motive to misrepresent may be shown to impeach the witness either by examination of the witness or by evidence otherwise adduced.

Note:

Except for the addition of subsection (c), this rule is identical to the federal rule.

Subsection (a) of this rule permits a witness' truthfulness to be impeached by opinion or reputation evidence. The general rule in South Carolina is that a witness' general reputation for truth and veracity is placed in issue when taking the witness stand. See State v. Major, 301 S.C. 181, 391 S.E.2d 235 (1990); State v. Robertson, 26 S.C. 117, 1 S.E. 443 (1887); State v. Hale, 284 S.C. 348, 326 S.E.2d 418 (Ct. App.1985), cert. denied, 286 S.C. 127, 332 S.E.2d 533 1985). Formerly, although evidence of a person's general reputation in the community was admissible, opinion testimony was not admissible. State v. Groome, 274 S.C. 189, 262 S.E.2d 31 (1980); In re: Greenfield's Estate, 245 S.C. 595, 141 S.E.2d 916 (1965). The provision prohibiting bolstering of a witness until after the witness' credibility is attacked is consistent with prior South Carolina law. State v. Lynn, 277 S.C. 222, 284 S.E.2d 786 (1981); Woods v. Thrower, 116 S.C. 165, 107 S.E. 250 (1921). However, there was an exception allowing bolstering prior to attack when the witness was a stranger to the community. State v. Lynn, supra; Woods v. Thrower, supra. This exception is not included in the rule.

As to subsection (b), no South Carolina cases have been found which permit cross-examination regarding specific acts to show truthfulness. The use of specific acts to attack credibility is similar to prior South Carolina case law which allowed a witness to be cross-examined about prior bad acts if they constituted crimes of moral turpitude. State v. Outlaw, 307 S.C. 177, 414 S.E.2d 147 (1992); State v. Major, 301 S.C. 181, 391 S.E.2d 235 (1990); State v. McGuire, 272 S.C. 547, 253 S.E.2d 103 (1979). The cross-examiner was required to take the answer given by the witness and could not use extrinsic evidence or other testimony to prove the bad act. State v. Outlaw, supra; State v. Major, supra. Additionally, the inquiry could only go so far as to bring out the general nature of the misconduct and could not go into specific details. State v. Outlaw, supra; State v. Major, supra.

Subsection (b), like its federal counterpart, does not set forth what conduct may adversely affect a witness' credibility. The former case law standard, which allowed impeachment if the conduct was a crime of moral turpitude, is not the appropriate standard in light of the Court's decision to abandon the moral turpitude standard under Rule 609. Instead, the trial courts should be guided by the decisions of the federal courts which limit inquiry into those specific instances of misconduct which are "clearly probative of truthfulness or untruthfulness" such as forgery, bribery, false pretenses, and embezzlement. See Weinstein's Evidence, 608[05] (1994). This will reduce the kinds of misconduct which can be inquired into from that permitted under prior law. Further, this rule, like the prior case law, does not allow a cross-examiner to go on a "fishing expedition" in the hopes of finding some misconduct. State v. McGuire, supra. The decision whether to allow such impeachment remains in the discretion of the trial judge. Id.

Subsection (c) was added to address impeachment by showing bias or impartiality. State v. Brewington, 267 S.C. 97, 226 S.E.2d 249 (1976); North Greenville College v. Sherman Const. Co., Inc., 270 S.C. 553, 243 S.E.2d 441 (1978).

Explanation

The purpose of impeachment is to undermine a witness's trustworthiness. This can be done by showing the witness is a known liar, they have a prior criminal record, they gave an inconsistent statement from what they are testifying today, they are biased, or several other ways. The question for the court is how can a party show that the witness is not trustworthy and at the same time, not lose focus on the trial at hand. The defendant is on trial, not the witness.

Rule 608 lays out three ways a witness can be impeached: their character, their conduct, or their bias.

Character

You can go after the witness's character by either opinion or reputation but this has to be about the witness's untruthfulness. If someone attacks the truthful character of a witness, then the other party can put up evidence (in form of opinion or reputation) that the person does have a truthful character. (You cannot bolster a witness's credibility at any point. They have to be attacked first).

Past Conduct

On cross examination, a party may ask the witness about specific conduct that makes them untrustworthy. This will be conduct that is probative of truthfulness or untruthfulness. But, that party cannot put up evidence if the witness denies it.

Bias

At any time, a party can put up evidence showing a witness is biased, prejudiced, or has a motive to misrepresent.

Case Law

"A witness may be impeached with evidence of '[b]ias, prejudice or any motive to misrepresent.' We recently held this rule 'preserves South Carolina precedent holding that

generally, anything having a legitimate tendency to throw light on the accuracy, truthfulness, and sincerity of a witness may be shown and considered in determining the credit to be accorded his testimony.' 'On cross-examination, any *fact* may be elicited which tends to show interest, bias, or partiality of the witness.'"
State v. Saltz, 346 S.C. 114, 131–32 (2001) (citation omitted)

Character

"These principles are incorporated into Rule 608(a) of the South Carolina Rules of Evidence. The rule provides that opinion evidence regarding credibility 'may refer only to character for truthfulness or untruthfulness,' and 'evidence of truthful character is admissible only after the character of the witness for truthfulness has been attacked by opinion or reputation evidence or otherwise.' Even a witness permitted to give an opinion under Rule 608(a) must restrict the opinion to 'character for truthfulness,' and may not testify whether the witness believes a specific statement or account given by another witness. *See* 1 Kenneth S. Broun et al., *McCormick on Evidence* § 43, at 205 (6th ed. 2006) (stating in relation to Rule 608(a), FRE, 'the opinion must relate to the prior witness's character trait for [ ]truthfulness, not the question of whether the witness's specific trial testimony was truthful'). Thus, to the extent Smith's testimony included comments on the credibility of the victim's account of the alleged sexual assault, the trial court erred in admitting it."
State v. McKerley, 397 S.C. 461, 464–65 (Ct. App. 2012)

Past Conduct

"The inquiry under Rule 608(b) is limited to those specific instances of misconduct which are clearly probative of truthfulness or untruthfulness such as forgery, bribery, false pretenses, and embezzlement."

State v. Quattlebaum, 338 S.C. 441, 450 (2000) (citation omitted)

Bias

"Under Rule 608(c), '[b]ias, prejudice or any motive to misrepresent may be shown to impeach the witness either by examination of the witness or by evidence otherwise adduced.' This subsection of Rule 608 preserves South Carolina precedent holding that generally, 'anything having a legitimate tendency to throw light on the accuracy, truthfulness, and sincerity of a witness may be shown and considered in determining the credit to be accorded his testimony.' "
State v. Jones, 343 S.C. 562, 570 (2001) (citation omitted)

RULE 609

IMPEACHMENT BY EVIDENCE OF CONVICTION OF
CRIME

(a) General Rule. For the purpose of attacking the credibility
of a witness,

> **(1)** evidence that a witness other than an accused has
> been convicted of a crime shall be admitted, subject
> to Rule 403, if the crime was punishable by death or
> imprisonment in excess of one year under the law
> under which the witness was convicted, and evidence
> that an accused has been convicted of such a crime
> shall be admitted if the court determines that the
> probative value of admitting this evidence outweighs
> its prejudicial effect to the accused; and

> **(2)** evidence that any witness has been convicted of a
> crime shall be admitted if it involved dishonesty or
> false statement, regardless of the punishment.

> For the purposes of this rule, a conviction includes a
> conviction resulting from a trial or any type of plea,
> including a plea of nolo contendere or a plea pursuant
> to North Carolina v. Alford, 400 U.S. 25 (1970).

(b) Time Limit. Evidence of a conviction under this rule is
not admissible if a period of more than ten years has elapsed
since the date of the conviction or of the release of the witness
from the confinement imposed for that conviction, whichever
is the later date, unless the court determines, in the interests of
justice, that the probative value of the conviction supported by
specific facts and circumstances substantially outweighs its

prejudicial effect. However, evidence of a conviction more than 10 years old as calculated herein, is not admissible unless the proponent gives to the adverse party sufficient advance written notice of intent to use such evidence to provide the adverse party with a fair opportunity to contest the use of such evidence.

(c) Effect of Pardon, Annulment, or Certificate of Rehabilitation or Other Equivalent Procedure. Evidence of a conviction is not admissible under this rule if (1) the conviction has been the subject of a pardon, annulment, certificate of rehabilitation, or other equivalent procedure based on a finding of the rehabilitation of the person convicted, and that person has not been convicted of a subsequent crime which was punishable by death or imprisonment in excess of one year, or (2) the conviction has been the subject of a pardon, annulment, or other equivalent procedure based on a finding of innocence.

(d) Juvenile Adjudications. Evidence of a juvenile adjudication is admissible under this rule if conviction of the crime would be admissible to attack the credibility of an adult.

(e) Pendency of Appeal. The pendency of an appeal therefrom does not render evidence of a conviction inadmissible. Evidence of the pendency of an appeal is admissible.

Note:

Except for subsections (a) and (d), this rule is identical to the federal rule.

Subsection (a) is identical to the federal rule except for the addition of the last sentence. This addition was made to make it clear that the term "conviction" includes a conviction resulting from a trial or any type of plea, to include a plea of *nolo contendere* or a plea pursuant to *North Carolina v. Alford*, 400 U.S. 25, 91 S.Ct. 160, 27 L.Ed.2d 162 (1970). Allowing a plea of *nolo contendere* to be used for impeachment is consistent with the prior law. *State v. Lynn*, 277 S.C. 222, 284 S.E.2d 786 (1981). Subsection (a) does change the law in South Carolina. The prior law was that a witness could be impeached by evidence that the witness had been convicted of a crime of moral turpitude. *State v. Hale*, 284 S.C. 348, 326 S.E.2d 418 (Ct.App.1985), *cert. denied*, 286 S.C. 127, 332 S.E.2d 533 (1985); *State v. Harvey*, 275 S.C. 225, 268 S.E.2d 587 (1980). Further, the standard for balancing probative value against prejudicial effect was the same for all witnesses, to include the accused in a criminal case. *Green v. Hewett*, 305 S.C. 238, 407 S.E.2d 651 (1991). This subsection does not use the moral turpitude standard, but instead allows impeachment with a conviction for any crime which carries a maximum sentence of death or imprisonment for more than one year. Further, the rule provides for a different standard for balancing probative value and prejudicial effect for an accused who is a witness.

Regarding subsection (b), the adoption of a general ten year limit on the use of convictions for impeachment constitutes a change in South Carolina law. The former case law did not set forth a time limit on the use of convictions for impeachment. *Green v. Hewett*, supra. Instead, the determination whether a conviction was too remote rested in the discretion of the trial judge. *Horton v. State*, 306 S.C. 252, 411 S.E.2d 223 (1991); *State v. Livingston*, 282 S.C. 1, 317 S.E.2d 129 (1984); *State v. Johnson*, 271 S.C. 485, 248 S.E.2d 313 (1978). The ten year limit was adopted to help guide trial courts in making uniform determinations in this area.

Subsection (c) regulates the effect of a pardon, annulment, certificate of rehabilitation or other equivalent procedures on the admissibility of a conviction for impeachment purposes. As to the effect of pardons issued by South Carolina, this subsection is arguably more restrictive than S.C. Code Ann. § 24-21-990(5) (Supp. 1993) which provides that a witness cannot be impeached by a conviction for which the witness received a pardon unless the crime indicates a lack of veracity.

The language of subsection (d) of the federal rule, which allows evidence of juvenile adjudications only in criminal cases and does not allow such evidence against the accused, was not used so that the South Carolina rule would conform with state law. Juvenile adjudications are admissible in this state to impeach any witness, including the accused, if the conduct would be criminal if it were committed by an adult. State v. Mallory, 270 S.C. 519, 242 S.E.2d 693 (1978). It should be noted that S.C. Code Ann. § 20-7-780 (Supp. 1993), which makes juvenile records confidential unless otherwise ordered by the family court, may limit access to records of juvenile adjudications.

No South Carolina authority existed as to the effect of the pendency of an appeal on the admissibility of evidence of the conviction. Subsection (e) of the federal rule was adopted verbatim.

Explanation

You can bring up a witness's prior conviction to impeach if:

- ❖ Carries over 1 year in prison (must also make 403 finding: prejudicial v. probative)

❖ Crime of dishonesty (comes in automatically, no 403)

❖ Can't bring it up if 10 years has passed since either conviction or release (whichever is later). However, if 10 years has passed then the court may let it in under certain circumstances. Must give notice.

Case Law

"Thus, we hold that for impeachment purposes, crimes of 'dishonesty or false statement' are crimes in the nature of *crimen falsi* 'that bear upon a witness's propensity to testify truthfully.' *United States v. Smith,* 551 F.2d 348, 362–63 (D.C.Cir.1976) ('[I]n its broadest sense, the term '*crimen falsi*' has encompassed only those crimes characterized by an element of deceit or deliberate interference with a court's ascertainment of truth.' (emphasis added)). Armed robbery, therefore, is not per se probative of truthfulness."
State v. Broadnax, 414 S.C. 468, 476, (2015) (citation omitted)

"Although the convictions arguably raise a concern as to Bush's general character, it is more narrowly his propensity for telling the truth, i.e., his credibility, that is properly placed at issue under Rule 609(b). The rule allows impeachment of a witness only as to his or her credibility, not as to all aspects of the witness's character. *See State v. Ross,* 329 N.C. 108, 405 S.E.2d 158, 165 (1991) (In applying the 'critical balancing process [of Rule 609(b)] it is important to remember that the only legitimate purpose for introducing evidence of past convictions is to *impeach the witness's credibility,*' not the witness's general character, and '[t]he use of this rule is necessarily limited by that focus.' (citation omitted))."
State v. Black, 400 S.C. 10, 23, 732 S.E.2d 880, 887 (2012)

"However, convictions that are over ten years old can be admitted 'in the interests of justice' if the trial court determines 'that the probative value of the conviction ... *substantially* outweighs its prejudicial effect.' Rule 609(b) (emphasis added). The trial court should consider the following factors in determining whether the probative value of a prior conviction outweighs its prejudicial effect: (1) the impeachment value of the prior crime; (2) the point in time of the conviction and the witness's subsequent history; (3) the similarity between the past crime and the charged crime; (4) the importance of the defendant's testimony; and (5) the centrality of the credibility issue."
State v. Shands, 424 S.C. 106, 121, 817 S.E.2d 524, 532 (Ct. App. 2018), reh'g denied (Aug. 16, 2018)

"We follow the majority of jurisdictions in holding that probation and parole do not constitute 'confinement' for the purposes of Rule 609(b); confinement ends when a defendant is released from actual imprisonment."
State v. Shands, 424 S.C. 106, 123, 817 S.E.2d 524, 533 (Ct. App. 2018), reh'g denied (Aug. 16, 2018)

"However, we find the trial court did not err in admitting Shands's prior conviction because Shands opened the door to such evidence. '[O]therwise inadmissible evidence may be properly admitted when opposing counsel opens the door to that evidence.' *State v. Page*, 378 S.C. 476, 482, 663 S.E.2d 357, 360 (Ct. App. 2008). 'A party cannot complain of prejudice from evidence to which he opened the door.' "
State v. Shands, 424 S.C. 106, 124, 817 S.E.2d 524, 533 (Ct. App. 2018), reh'g denied (Aug. 16, 2018)

RULE 610
RELIGIOUS BELIEFS OR OPINIONS

Evidence of the beliefs or opinions of a witness on matters of religion is not admissible for the purpose of showing that by reason of their nature the witness' credibility is impaired or enhanced.

Note:

No changes were made to the language of the federal rule. The South Carolina Supreme Court has held that a belief in God is not a prerequisite to allowing the witness to testify. State v. Green, 267 S.C. 599, 230 S.E.2d 618 (1976); State v. Hicks, 257 S.C. 279, 185 S.E.2d 746 (1971). However, in State v. Turner, 36 S.C. 534, 15 S.E. 602 (1892), the State was allowed to question the accused concerning comments ridiculing religion which he had allegedly made in order to impeach his credibility. This case is inconsistent with the rule.

RULE 611

MODE AND ORDER OF INTERROGATION AND
PRESENTATION

(a) Control by Court. The court shall exercise reasonable
control over the mode and order of interrogating witnesses
and presenting evidence so as to (1) make the interrogation
and presentation effective for the ascertainment of the truth,
(2) avoid needless consumption of time, and (3) protect
witnesses from harassment or undue embarrassment.

(b) Scope of Cross-Examination. A witness may be cross-
examined on any matter relevant to any issue in the case,
including credibility.

(c) Leading Questions. Leading questions should not be used
on the direct examination of a witness except as may be
necessary to develop the witness' testimony. Ordinarily
leading questions should be permitted on cross-examination.
When a party calls a hostile witness, an adverse party, or a
witness identified with an adverse party, interrogation may be
by leading questions.

(d) Re-examination and Recall. A witness may be re-
examined as to the same matters to which he testified only in
the discretion of the court, but without exception he may be
re-examined as to any new matter brought out during cross-
examination. After the examination of the witness has been
concluded by all the parties to the action, that witness may be
recalled only in the discretion of the court. This rule shall not
limit the right of any party to recall a witness in rebuttal.

Note:

The language of subsection (a) of this rule is identical to that used in the federal rule. It is consistent with the general rule in this State that the conduct of the trial, including the examination of witnesses, is within the sound discretion of the trial judge. See McMillan v. Ridges, 229 S.C. 76, 91 S.E.2d 883 (1956); State v. Nathari, 303 S.C. 188, 399 S.E.2d 597 (Ct. App. 1990). It should be noted that Rule 614 controls the calling and interrogation of witnesses by the court.

Under South Carolina law, cross-examination is limited only by the requirement that the inquiry relate to matters pertinent to the issues involved or to impeachment of the witness. See State v. Ham, 259 S.C. 118, 191 S.E.2d 13 (1972); Hansson v. General Insulation and Acoustics, 234 S.C. 177, 107 S.E.2d 41 (1959). The scope of cross-examination is within the discretion of the trial judge. State v. Sherard, 303 S.C. 172, 399 S.E.2d 595 (1991). Subsection (b) rejects the more restrictive language of the federal rule which limits cross-examination to the subject matter of direct examination and matters affecting the credibility of the witness.

Subsection (c) is consistent with former law. See Rule 43(b)(1), SCRCP; Rule 43(b)(2), SCRCP. The use of leading questions when examining a child, State v. Hale, 284 S.C. 348, 326 S.E.2d 418 (Ct. App. 1985), cert. denied, 286 S.C. 127, 332 S.E.2d 533 (1985), is still permissible under the first sentence of subsection (c) which allows leading questions when "necessary to develop the witness' testimony."

There was no provision in the federal rule as to re-examination and recall of witnesses. The provision concerning re-examination and recall of witnesses was added to the rule to make it consistent with South Carolina law. SeeLevy v. Outdoor Resorts of South Carolina, Inc., 304

S.C. 427, 405 S.E.2d 387 (1991); State v. Stroman, 281 S.C. 508, 316 S.E.2d 395 (1984); Huff v. Latimer, 33 S.C. 255, 11 S.E. 758 (1890).

Case Law

" 'A witness may be cross-examined on any matter relevant to any issue in the case, including credibility.' Rule 611(b), SCRE. Considerable latitude is allowed in cross-examination to test a witness's credibility. *Martin v. Dunlap,* 266 S.C. 230, 222 S.E.2d 8 (1976). However, a trial judge may impose reasonable limits on cross-examination based upon concerns about, among other things, harassment, prejudice, confusion of the issues, witness safety, or interrogation that is repetitive or only marginally relevant. *State v. Jenkins,* 322 S.C. 360, 474 S.E.2d 812 (Ct.App.1996). An appellate court will not disturb a trial court's ruling concerning the scope of cross-examination of a witness to test his or her credibility, or to show possible bias or self-interest in testifying, absent a manifest abuse of discretion."
State v. Johnson, 338 S.C. 114, 124–25, 525 S.E.2d 519, 524 (2000)

"First, the trial court's limitation on how much of the audiotape was played to the jury was partially based on trial management. This was within the judge's discretion under Rule 611(a), SCRE.[7] Chase argued that the conversations were offered only to demonstrate the tone and nature of the communications between Chase and the victim. The trial judge explained, '[w]ell, we don't need to hear the whole tape to hear their tones. I mean, I've heard enough to know what their tone is with one another.' "
State v. Chase, No. 2011-UP-210, 2011 WL 11734321, at *6 (S.C. Ct. App. May 11, 2011)

"Second, Chase argues that the trial judge's ruling interfered with his ability to prove that the victim had a motive to lie about the choking and fisting incident. However, we find Chase was able to elicit ample testimony from Lynch about her conspiracy with the victim to lie about Chase in order to influence the custody dispute over Kalei. Further, the trial court's decision to exclude wide-ranging testimony about conduct of the parties during the custody battle was within her discretion under Rule 611(a), SCRE."
State v. Chase, No. 2011-UP-210, 2011 WL 11734321, at *7 (S.C. Ct. App. May 11, 2011)

Rule of completeness

"We find the common law of this state extends the rule of completeness to oral communications. *Jackson, supra. Accord State v. Eugenio,* 219 Wis.2d 391, 579 N.W.2d 642 (1998) (notwithstanding provision identical to Rule 106 referring only to written or recorded statements, common law rule of completeness continues to exist for oral statements); *State v. Cruz–Meza,* 76 P.3d 1165 (Utah 2003) (recognizing rule of completeness may be applied to oral statements through Rule 611);[3] *State v. Johnson,* 479 A.2d 1284 (Maine 1984). *See also United States v. Haddad,* 10 F.3d 1252 (7th Cir.1993) (citing 1 Weinstein & Berger, *Weinstein's Evidence,* § 106–4 (1992)). Accordingly, where, as here, the state elects to use a witness to elicit portions of a conversation (and incriminating statements therein) made by a defendant, the rule of completeness requires the defendant be permitted to inquire into the full substance of that conversation."
State v. Cabrera-Pena, 361 S.C. 372, 380, 605 S.E.2d 522, 526 (2004)

RULE 612
WRITING USED TO REFRESH MEMORY

If a witness uses a writing to refresh memory for the purpose of testifying, either -

>   **(1)** while testifying, or

>   **(2)** before testifying, if the court in its discretion determines it is necessary in the interests of justice,

an adverse party is entitled to have the writing produced at the hearing, to inspect it, to cross-examine the witness thereon, and to introduce in evidence those portions which relate to the testimony of the witness. If it is claimed that the writing contains matters not related to the subject matter of the testimony the court shall examine the writing in camera, excise any portions not so related, and order delivery of the remainder to the party entitled thereto. Any portion withheld over objections shall be preserved and made available to the appellate court in the event of an appeal. If a writing is not produced or delivered pursuant to order under this rule, the court shall make any order justice requires, except that in criminal cases when the prosecution elects not to comply, the order shall be one striking the testimony or, if the court in its discretion determines that the interests of justice so require, declaring a mistrial.

Note:

Except for the deletion of a reference to federal law, no changes were made to the federal rule. Requiring a party to provide a copy of a memorandum used by a witness to refresh recollection so that it may be used on cross-examination of the witness is consistent with prior law. State v. Hamilton, 276 S.C. 173, 276 S.E.2d 784 (1981); State v. Tyner, 273 S.C. 646, 258 S.E.2d 559 (1979). Rule 37(b)(2), SCRCP, and Rule 5(d)(2), SCRCrimP, are similar to the provision in this rule concerning the trial judge's authority to decide the remedy for failure to produce a document for the adverse party.

Explanation

This method is used when a witness is having troubling remembering a certain thing while on the stand.

> First: The witness claims they are having trouble remembering a certain thing.

> Second: The attorney asks them if a writing would help refresh their memory.

> Third: The attorney gives a copy of the writing to both the witness and the other attorney.

> Fourth: After the witness looks over the writing, the attorney asks them if their memory is refreshed.

Remember, the witness does not get to simply read the writing word for word out loud to the jury (unless the writing falls under the hearsay exception 803(5)).

Also remember, the attorney who used the writing to refresh his witness's memory does not get to submit the writing as evidence. The opposing party may submit it though.

Case Law

"While the State seems to suggest that the photo was admissible because it used the photo to refresh Wife's

memory, this argument is unsupported by law. *See* Rule 612, SCRE (stating that a writing used to refresh
memory may be introduced into evidence by an *adverse* party in the trial court's discretion, as necessary to serve the interest of justice) (emphasis added)."
State v. Watkins, No. 2009-UP-402, 2009 WL 9529410, at *4 (S.C. Ct. App. Aug. 12, 2009)

"During trial, the State called Crystal Tuck as an expert in child sexual abuse treatment and counseling. She testified the victim's behavior was consistent with child sexual abuse. On cross-examination, Hughes asked if Tuck had reviewed her notes before testifying. Tuck responded she had used her notes to refresh her memory. Hughes then sought to inspect the notes pursuant to Rule 612, SCRE. The trial court refused to require Tuck to submit those notes because they were in Columbia and the trial was being held in Orangeburg. The trial court also refused to require Tuck to submit the notes prior to the end of the trial so Hughes could proffer them...
Here, Tuck's testimony on cross-examination demonstrates she relied on her notes to refresh her memory before trial. Initially, the trial court was inclined to admit the notes, but after discovering the notes were in Columbia rather than in Orangeburg, it refused to require their submission for inspection or proffer. The trial court apparently believed it was powerless to order Tuck to produce anything that was not in the courtroom. This was an error of law because the rule's language is not limited to materials located inside the courtroom. Therefore, the trial court erred in failing to exercise its discretion."
State v. Hughes, 346 S.C. 339, 343 (Ct. App. 2001) (citation omitted)

RULE 613
PRIOR STATEMENTS OF WITNESSES

Subject to the provisions of S.C. Code Ann. §§ 19-1-80, 19-1-90 and 19-1-100:

(a) Examining Witness Concerning Prior Statement. In examining a witness concerning a prior statement made by the witness, whether written or not, the statement need not be shown nor its contents disclosed to the witness at that time, but on request the same shall be shown or disclosed to opposing counsel.

(b) Extrinsic Evidence of Prior Inconsistent Statement of Witness. Extrinsic evidence of a prior inconsistent statement by a witness is not admissible unless the witness is advised of the substance of the statement, the time and place it was allegedly made, and the person to whom it was made, and is given the opportunity to explain or deny the statement. If a witness does not admit that he has made the prior inconsistent statement, extrinsic evidence of such statement is admissible. However, if a witness admits making the prior statement, extrinsic evidence that the prior statement was made is inadmissible. This provision does not apply to admissions of a party-opponent as defined in Rule 801(d)(2).

Note:

The language at the beginning of this rule was added to provide that the rule is subject to the provisions of S.C. Code Ann. §§ 19-1-80 to -100 (1985) regarding written statements made to public employees.

Subsection (a) is identical to the federal rule. This provision was included in the federal rule to abolish the holding in The Queen's Case, 2 Br. & B. 284, 129 Eng. Rep. 976 (1820), that a witness must be shown a prior statement before being examined about the statement. Although no South Carolina case has been found adopting the holding in The Queen's Case, the language of the federal rule eliminating the requirement of showing the witness the prior statement has been included in the South Carolina rule.

Subsection (b) of the federal rule was amended to provide that a proper foundation must be laid before admitting a prior inconsistent statement. A witness must be permitted to admit, deny, or explain a prior inconsistent statement. McMillan v. Ridges, 229 S.C. 76, 91 S.E.2d 883 (1956). Extrinsic evidence of the statement is not admissible unless the witness is advised of the substance of the statement, the time and place it was allegedly made, and the person to whom it was made. State v. Galloway, 263 S.C. 585, 211 S.E.2d 885 (1975). In addition, language was added to subsection (b) to set forth the rule that if the witness admits making the prior statement, the witness has been impeached and no further extrinsic evidence of the statement, including the statement itself, is admissible. State v. Lynn, 277 S.C. 222, 284 S.E.2d 786 (1981); McMillan v. Ridges, supra.

Explanation

You have to lay a foundation before you can try and get in a statement (substance, time, place). If the defendant denies ever making that statement, then you can bring in evidence that they in fact did give that statement.

Case Law

"Once the State confronted Ms. Barnes with the substance of her previous statement, the time and place it was made, and the person to whom it was made, and she denied making it, the foundation required by Rule 613(b) was complete...The rule does not require extrinsic evidence of the prior statement be admitted immediately. It merely authorizes the use of extrinsic evidence to prove the inconsistency. Because the impeaching evidence is 'extrinsic,' the avenue of its admissibility may not always run through the witness to be impeached by it, for that witness may not be competent to authenticate the extrinsic evidence."
State v. Barnes, 421 S.C. 47, 57–58 (Ct. App. 2017)

"The record clearly reflects that Rita admitted having the conversation at issue but specifically denied making the statements later testified to by Taylor. Thus, the State laid a proper foundation under Rule 613(b), SCRE, and we find that Appellant's argument is entirely without merit."
State v. Bixby, 388 S.C. 528, 552 (2010).

"It is mandatory that a witness be permitted to admit, deny, or explain a prior inconsistent statement. Under Rule 613(b), extrinsic evidence of the statement is not admissible unless the witness is advised of the substance of the statement, the time and place it was allegedly made, and the person to whom it was made. Rule 613(b) explicates the procedure for impeachment by a prior inconsistent statement and requires laying the foundation...Consequently, the trial judge did not abuse his discretion in excluding the testimony due to the failure to provide a sufficient foundation under Rule 613(b)."
State v. McLeod, 362 S.C. 73, 81 (Ct. App. 2004)

"Unlike the federal rule, the South Carolina rule requires that a proper foundation must be laid before admitting

a prior inconsistent statement. *State v. McLeod,* 362 S.C. 73, 81, 606 S.E.2d 215, 219 (Ct.App.2004). Thus, '[i]t is mandatory that a witness be permitted to admit, deny, or explain a prior inconsistent statement.' *Id.*"
State v. Moses, 390 S.C. 502, 522, 702 S.E.2d 395, 406 (Ct. App. 2010)

"The trial court did not err in allowing Coach Robert Searfoss to testify regarding Gahagan's prior inconsistent statement. 'Generally, where the witness has responded with anything less than an unequivocal admission, trial courts have been granted wide latitude to allow extrinsic evidence proving the statement.' *State v. Blalock,* 357 S.C. 74, 80, 591 S.E.2d 632, 636 (Ct.App.2003); *see also State v. Carmack,* 388 S.C. 190, 201–02, 694 S.E.2d 224, 230 (Ct.App.2010) (holding witness did not unequivocally admit making a prior inconsistent statement; therefore, the trial court did not abuse its discretion in allowing extrinsic evidence of the statement). This wide latitude extends to a witness indicating an inability to recall or to remember a previous statement:

> If the witness neither directly admit[s] nor den[ies] the act or declaration, as when he merely says that he does not recollect, or, as it seems, gives any other indirect answer not amounting to an admission, it is competent for the adversary to prove the affirmative, for otherwise the witness might in every such case exclude evidence of what he had done or said by answering that he did not remember."

State v. Moses, 390 S.C. 502, 522–23, 702 S.E.2d 395, 406 (Ct. App. 2010)

RULE 614
CALLING AND INTERROGATION OF WITNESSES BY
COURT

(a) Calling by Court, In extraordinary circumstances, the court may, on its own motion or at the suggestion of a party, call witnesses, and all parties are entitled to cross-examine witnesses thus called. Before calling a court's witness, the court shall afford the parties a hearing on the matter outside the presence of the jury.

(b) Interrogation by Court. When required by the interests of justice only, the court may interrogate witnesses.

Note:

Subsection (a) is the federal rule modified in two respects. First, the phrase "[i]n extraordinary circumstances" was added to emphasize that under our adversarial system the decision whether to call a witness should generally be made by the parties, and the power of the court to call a witness ought to be sparingly used. The formulation of this rule differs from the rule established in State v. Anderson, 304 S.C. 551, 406 S.E.2d 152 (1991), although the circumstances in that case would be extraordinary circumstances justifying a court in calling a witness under this rule. Second, the federal rule was modified to require the court to afford the parties a hearing outside the presence of the jury before a witness is called by the court. This modification is consistent with prior case law. Id.; Riddle v. State, 314 S.C. 1, 443 S.E.2d 557 (1994). Allowing all parties to cross-examine a court's witness is also consistent with the prior case law. Riddle v. State, supra; State v. Anderson, supra.

Subsection (b) is the federal rule modified by adding the phrase "[w]hen required by the interests of justice only." This language was added to emphasize that this power, like the power to call a court's witness, should be used sparingly. If the court does interrogate a witness, the court must be careful not to intimate any opinion as to the force and effect of the testimony by its questions. Fowler v. Laney Tank Lines, Inc., *263 S.C. 422, 211 S.E.2d 231 (1975).*

The federal rule contains a subsection (c) which may obviate the need for a timely objection to the calling of a court's witness or the interrogation of a witness by the court in certain circumstances. This provision is inconsistent with the law of South Carolina and was deleted. See State v. Torrence, *305 S.C. 45, 406 S.E.2d 315 (1991).*

Case Law

"The testimony provided by Crosby, as compared with Miller's prior filings with the probate court, indicates a discrepancy in his representations to the probate court. We find these circumstances are extraordinary and meet the requirements pursuant to Rule 614, SCRE, allowing the probate court to call an additional witness. In addition, the probate court afforded both parties notice of Clark's testimony and the opportunity to cross-examine her, and therefore, neither was prejudiced by her testimony."
Dep't of Health & Human Serv. v. Miller, No. 2005-UP-154, 2005 WL 7083832, at *5 (S.C. Ct. App. Mar. 1, 2005)

RULE 615
EXCLUSION OF WITNESSES

At the request of a party the court may order witnesses excluded so that they cannot hear the testimony of other witnesses, and it may make the order of its own motion. This rule does not authorize exclusion of (1) a party who is a natural person, or (2) an officer or employee of a party which is not a natural person designated as its representative by its attorney, or (3) a person whose presence is shown by a party to be essential to the presentation of the party's cause.

Note:

The federal rule requires sequestration of witnesses upon the request of a party. The South Carolina rule adheres to prior state practice which leaves the sequestration decision in the sound discretion of the trial judge. SeeState v. Jackson, 265 S.C. 278, 217 S.E.2d 794 (1975); State v. Miokovich, 257 S.C. 225, 185 S.E.2d 360 (1971). Otherwise, the South Carolina rule is consistent with the federal rule.

Case Law

" 'The purpose of the exclusion rule is, of course, to prevent the possibility of one witness shaping his testimony to match that given by other witnesses at the trial; and if a witness violates the order he may be disciplined by the court. The question of the exclusion of the testimony of the offending witness, however, depends upon the particular circumstances and lies within the sound discretion of the trial court.' *U.S. v. Leggett,* 326 F.2d 613, 613–14 (4th Cir.1964). A circuit court may order the sequestration of any witness by order or by

motion of a party. Rule 615, SCRE. However, a party is not entitled to have witnesses sequestered as a matter of right;[5] instead, the decision to sequester a witness is within the sound discretion of the circuit court."
State v. Huckabee, 388 S.C. 232, 241, 694 S.E.2d 781, 785 (Ct. App. 2010)

" 'Rather, the decision to sequester witnesses is left to the sound discretion of the trial judge.' *Id.* 'This discretion extends to the State's right to recall a witness in reply who was present in the courtroom during a portion of the trial.' *Id.*
'Whether a witness should be exempted from a sequestration order is within the trial court's discretion.' *State v. Tisdale,* 338 S.C. 607, 616, 527 S.E.2d 389, 394 (Ct.App.2000) (declining to grant a mistrial based on violation of a sequestration order by the State's witness); *see also Fulton,* 333 S.C. at 375, 509 S.E.2d at 827 (finding no abuse of discretion by the trial judge in allowing reply testimony from two previously sequestered witnesses who had remained in the courtroom following their initial testimony). Moreover, '[t]he admission of reply testimony is within the sound discretion of the trial judge, and there is no abuse of discretion if the testimony is arguably contradictory of and in reply to earlier testimony.' *State v. Todd,* 290 S.C. 212, 214, 349 S.E.2d 339, 340 (1986); *see also State v. Huckabee,* 388 S.C. 232, 243, 694 S.E.2d 781, 786 (Ct.App.2010) (finding no abuse of discretion by the trial judge in allowing reply testimony when it was limited in scope to contradict a previous contention raised by the defendant and not admitted to complete the State's case-in-chief)."
State v. Singleton, 395 S.C. 6, 15–16, 716 S.E.2d 332, 337 (Ct. App. 2011)

Article VII. Opinions and Expert Testimony

RULE 701
OPINION TESTIMONY BY LAY WITNESSES

If the witness is not testifying as an expert, the witness' testimony in the form of opinions or inferences is limited to those opinions or inferences which (a) are rationally based on the perception of the witness, (b) are helpful to a clear understanding of the witness' testimony or the determination of a fact in issue, and (c) do not require special knowledge, skill, experience or training.

Note:

Except for the addition of subsection (c) and minor grammatical changes, this rule is identical to the federal rule. The language of subsection (c) is based on language contained in the rules of evidence of Florida and Tennessee, and is intended to emphasize the fact that lay persons may not give expert opinions.

Subsection (a) appears to be consistent with prior law. Cf. State v. Bottoms, 260 S.C. 187, 195 S.E.2d 116 (1973) (opinion must be based upon the personal observations of the witness and not merely upon the statements of another witness).

As to subsection (b), the prior case law has held that opinion evidence is admissible as long as it is not superfluous. State v. McClinton, 265 S.C. 171, 217 S.E.2d 584 (1974). This is roughly equivalent to saying that opinion evidence must be helpful.

As to subsection (c), the Court of Appeals has stated that expert testimony is essential where the topic is not a matter within the common knowledge and experience of most lay persons. Spartanburg Regional Med.Center v. Bulsa, 308 S.C. 322, 417 S.E.2d 648 (Ct. App. 1992); Armstrong v. Union Carbide, 308 S.C. 235, 417 S.E.2d 597 (Ct. App. 1992). Subsection (c) merely states this proposition in the reverse.

Case Law

"We find the trial court abused its discretion by committing an error of law when it admitted Clevenger's testimony regarding the cause of Victim's death because it constituted improper opinion testimony from a lay witness. Clevenger's opinion as to Victim's cause of death was not based on his perceptions. *See* Rule 701(a)
(requiring opinion testimony from a lay witness be limited to opinions based on the witness's perceptions). Clevenger testified his determination of Victim's cause of death was based on the findings of the pathologist and the investigation of law enforcement. Thus, Clevenger's opinion regarding the cause of Victim's death was not based on his perceptions or observations but instead was based on his review of the perceptions of others. As a result, his testimony as a lay witness was improper opinion testimony under Rule 701(a).[1] *See Douglas*, 380 S.C. at 502–03, 671 S.E.2d at 608 (finding the trial court was not required to qualify the witness as an expert because she testified only to her personal observations and experiences); *Small v. Pioneer Machinery, Inc.*, 329 S.C. 448, 468, 494 S.E.2d 835, 845 (Ct. App. 1997) (finding a lay witness could offer his opinion as to what caused a machine to malfunction because his opinion was based 'upon his observations and perceptions as the [daily] operator' of the machine)."

State v. Westmoreland, 421 S.C. 410, 419–20, 807 S.E.2d 701, 706–07 (Ct. App. 2017), reh'g denied (Dec. 14, 2017)

"On the other hand, a lay witness may only testify as to matters within his personal knowledge and may not offer opinion testimony which requires special knowledge, skill, experience, or training. *See* Rules 602 and 701, SCRE." Watson v. Ford Motor Co., 389 S.C. 434, 446, 699 S.E.2d 169, 175 (2010)

"The opinion or inference of a lay witness is admissible if it is a) rationally based on the perception of the witness, b) helpful to the determination of a fact in issue, and c) does not require special knowledge. Rule 701, SCRE. *See also* 31 A Am.Jur.2d *Expert and Opinion Evidence* § 30; 23 C.J.S. *Criminal Law* § 1050. Conclusions or opinions of laymen should be rejected only when they are superfluous in the sense that they will be of no value to the jury. *State v. McClinton,* 265 S.C. 171, 217 S.E.2d 584 (1975). The terms 'fact' and 'opinion' denote merely a difference of degree of concreteness of description. *McCormick on Evidence,* § 12 (3rd Ed.1984). Some statements are not mere opinions but are impressions drawn from collected, observed facts. *Lafon v. Commonwealth,* 17 Va.App. 411, 438 S.E.2d 279 (1993). A natural inference based on stated facts is not opinion evidence. *State v. Revere,* 572 So.2d 117 (La.App.1990). Where the distinction between fact and opinion is blurred, it is often best to leave the matter to the discretion of the trial judge."
State v. Williams, 321 S.C. 455, 463–64, 469 S.E.2d 49, 54 (1996)

RULE 702
TESTIMONY BY EXPERTS

If scientific, technical, or other specialized knowledge will assist the trier of fact to understand the evidence or to determine a fact in issue, a witness qualified as an expert by knowledge, skill, experience, training, or education, may testify thereto in the form of an opinion or otherwise.

Note:

The rule is identical to the federal rule, and to former Rule 43(m)(1), SCRCP, and former Rule 24(a), SCRCrimP.

Explanation

Before an expert may testify, a judge needs to make preliminary findings:

1. Subject matter is beyond ordinary knowledge of jury.
2. The expert must be qualified in that particular field.
3. The substance of the testimony must be reliable.
   a. *Scientific in nature*:
      i. Publications/peer reviews.
      ii. Prior application of the method to the type of evidence.
      iii. Quality control measures.
      iv. The consistency of the method with recognized scientific laws and procedures.
   b. *Nonscientific in nature*:

i. No set test. Judge must still play
gatekeeper though.

Case Law

"For these reasons, expert testimony receives additional
scrutiny relative to other evidentiary decisions. Specifically,
in executing its gatekeeping duties, the trial court must make
three key preliminary findings which are fundamental to Rule
702 before the jury may consider expert testimony. **First**, the
trial court must find that the subject matter is beyond the
ordinary knowledge of the jury, thus requiring an expert to
explain the matter to the jury. *See State v. Douglas,* 380 S.C.
499, 671 S.E.2d 606 (2009) (holding that the witness was
improperly qualified as a forensic interviewing expert where
the nature of her testimony was based on personal
observations and discussions with the child victim). **Next**,
while the expert need not be a specialist in the particular
branch of the field, the trial court must find that the proffered
expert has indeed acquired the requisite knowledge and skill
to qualify as an expert in the particular subject
matter. *See Gooding v. St. Francis Xavier Hosp.,* 326 S.C.
248, 252–53, 487 S.E.2d 596, 598 (1997) (observing that to
be competent to testify as an expert, a witness must have
acquired by reason of study or experience such knowledge
and skill in a profession or science that he is better qualified
than the jury to form an opinion on the particular subject of
his testimony). **Finally**, the trial court must evaluate the
substance of the testimony and determine whether it is
reliable. *See State v. Council,* 335 S.C. 1, 20, 515 S.E.2d 508,
518 (evaluating whether expert testimony on DNA analysis
met the reliability requirements).
Expert testimony is not admissible unless it satisfies all three
requirements with respect to subject matter, expert
qualifications, and reliability. Thus, only after the trial court

has found that expert testimony is necessary to assist the jury in resolving factual questions, the expert is qualified in the particular area, and the testimony is reliable, may the trial court admit the evidence and permit the jury to assign it such weight as it deems appropriate."
Watson v. Ford Motor Co., 389 S.C. 434, 446–47, 699 S.E.2d 169, 175 (2010) (emphasis added)

"White concedes the dog handler met the Rule 702, SCRE, qualifications due to his experience and training.[3] White contends the trial court failed in its gatekeeping role to vet the reliability of the dog's tracking skills, thus leaving the jury to speculate about the dog's reliability. We agree with White's premise that all expert testimony under Rule 702, SCRE, imposes on the trial courts an affirmative and meaningful gatekeeping duty. To the extent the court of appeals opinion may be construed as excluding a gatekeeping role for trial courts in connection with nonscientific (or experienced based)[4] expert testimony, such construction is rejected."
State v. White, 382 S.C. 265, 269–70, 676 S.E.2d 684, 686 (2009)

"All expert testimony must meet the requirements of Rule 702, regardless of whether it is scientific, technical, or otherwise. The qualification of a witness as an expert is within the discretion of the circuit court, and we will not reverse absent an abuse of that discretion."
Graves v. CAS Med. Sys., Inc., 401 S.C. 63, 74, 735 S.E.2d 650, 655 (2012) (citation omitted)

Scientific vs. nonscientific

"If the proffered testimony is scientific in nature, then the circuit court must determine its reliability per the factors set forth in *Council. Id.* at 449–50, 699 S.E.2d at 177. Under *Council,* the court must consider the following: '(1) the

publications and peer review of the technique; (2) prior application of the method to the type of evidence involved in the case; (3) the quality control procedures used to ensure reliability; and (4) the consistency of the method with recognized scientific laws and procedures.' 335 S.C. at 19, 515 S.E.2d at 517. However, these factors 'serve no useful analytical purpose' for nonscientific evidence. *White,* 382 S.C. at 274, 676 S.E.2d at 688. In those cases, we have declined to offer any specific factors for the circuit court to consider due to 'the myriad of Rule 702 qualification and reliability challenges that could arise with respect to nonscientific expert evidence.' *Id.* Nevertheless, the court must still exercise its role as gatekeeper and determine whether the proffered evidence is reliable. *Id.* Thus, while a challenge to an opinion's reliability generally goes to weight and not admissibility, this 'familiar evidentiary mantra' may not be invoked until the circuit court has vetted its reliability in the first instance and deemed the testimony admissible."
Graves v. CAS Med. Sys., Inc., 401 S.C. 63, 74–75, 735 S.E.2d 650, 655–56 (2012)

RULE 703
BASES OF OPINION TESTIMONY BY EXPERTS

The facts or data in the particular case upon which an expert bases an opinion or inference may be those perceived by or made known to the expert at or before the hearing. If of a type reasonably relied upon by experts in the particular field in forming opinions or inferences upon the subject, the facts or data need not be admissible in evidence.

Note:

The rule is identical to the federal rule and former Rule 43(m)(2), SCRCP, and former Rule 24(b), SCRCrimP. This rule makes it clear that an expert may rely on facts or data in giving an opinion which are not admitted into evidence.

Case Law

"Expert testimony may be used to help the jury to determine a fact in issue based on the expert's specialized knowledge, experience, or skill and is necessary in cases in which the subject matter falls outside the realm of ordinary lay knowledge. Stated differently, expert evidence is required where a factual issue must be resolved with scientific, technical, or any other specialized knowledge. Expert testimony differs from lay testimony in that an expert witness is permitted to state an opinion based on facts not within his firsthand knowledge or may base his opinion on information made available before the hearing so long as it is the type of information that is reasonably relied upon in the field to make opinions."

Watson v. Ford Motor Co., 389 S.C. 434, 445–46, 699 S.E.2d
169, 175 (2010)

"The defendants argue the trial court erred by allowing the
expert, under the guise of Rule 703, to act as a 'conduit' for
inadmissible hearsay. They contend the figures were not the
type of data relied upon by economists, but were instead
foundational facts which must be separately proved. In this
regard, they reason that Rule 703 is subservient to other Rules
of Evidence.

Disposing of this latter assertion first, we note that generally
under Rule 602, SCRE, '[a] witness may not testify to a matter
unless evidence is introduced sufficient to support a finding
that the witness has personal knowledge of the matter.'
However, this rule specifically states that it is subject to Rule
703. Consequently, we do not find Rule 703 to be subservient,
as argued by the defendants.

An expert witness may state an opinion based on facts not
within his firsthand knowledge. He may base his opinion on
information, whether or not admissible, made available to him
before the hearing if the information is of the type reasonably
relied upon in the field to make opinions. Also, an expert may
testify as to matters of hearsay for the purpose of showing
what information he relied on in giving his opinion of value."
Hundley ex rel. Hundley v. Rite Aid of S.C., Inc., 339 S.C.
285, 294–95, 529 S.E.2d 45, 50 (Ct. App. 2000) (citations
omitted)

RULE 704

OPINION ON ULTIMATE ISSUE

Testimony in the form of an opinion or inference otherwise admissible is not objectionable because it embraces an ultimate issue to be decided by the trier of fact.

Note:

This rule is identical to former Rule 43(m)(3), SCRCP, and former Rule 24(c), SCRCrimP. It is identical to the federal rule as it existed prior the 1984 amendment which added subsection (b) to the rule to prohibit expert testimony on the ultimate issue of whether a criminal defendant is insane.

Case Law

"Generally, '[t]estimony in the form of an opinion or inference otherwise admissible is not objectionable because it embraces an ultimate issue to be decided by the trier of fact.' Rule 704, SCRE. However, expert testimony on issues of law is usually inadmissible."
State v. Commander, 396 S.C. 254, 264, 721 S.E.2d 413, 418 (2011)

" 'Testimony in the form of an opinion or inference otherwise admissible is not objectionable because it embraces an ultimate issue to be decided by the trier of fact.' Rule 704, SCRE. However, an opinion may be offered on the ultimate issue of the case only when the witness is otherwise qualified. Likewise, an expert's testimony may not exceed the scope of his expertise."

State v. Andrews, 424 S.C. 304, 317–18, 818 S.E.2d 227, 234 (Ct. App. 2018), reh'g denied (Sept. 20, 2018) (citation omitted)

RULE 705
DISCLOSURE OF FACTS OR DATA UNDERLYING EXPERT OPINION

The expert may testify in terms of opinion or inference and give reasons therefor without first testifying to the underlying facts or data, unless the court requires otherwise. The expert may in any event be required to disclose the underlying facts or data on cross-examination.

Note:

The rule is identical to the federal rule. It differs from former Rule 43(m)(4), SCRCP, and former Rule 24(d), SCRCrimP, which contained the phrase "without prior disclosure of" in place of the phrase "without first testifying to."

Case Law

"The scope of a cross-examiner's right under Rule 705 is best stated in McCormick's treatise on evidence:

> On cross-examination in the process of probing the witness' qualifications, experience, bases, and assumptions opposing counsel may require the expert to disclose the facts, data, and opinions underlying the expert's opinion not previously disclosed. With respect to facts, data, or opinions forming the basis of the expert's opinion, disclosed on direct examination or during cross-examination, the cross-examiner may explore whether, and if so how, the non-

existence of any fact, data, or opinion or the existence of a contrary version of the fact, data, or opinion supported by the evidence, would affect the expert's opinion. Similarly the expert may be cross-examined with respect to material reviewed by the expert but upon which the expert does not rely. Counsel is also permitted to test the knowledge, experience, and fairness of the expert by inquiring as to what changes of conditions would affect his opinion, and in conducting such an inquiry, subject to the requirements of Fed.R.Evid. 403, the cross-examiner is not limited to facts finding support in the record.

Kenneth S. Broun et al., *McCormick on Evidence* § 13, at 56-57 (John William Strong ed., 4th ed. 1992)."

State v. Slocumb, 336 S.C. 619, 628, 521 S.E.2d 507, 512 (Ct. App. 1999)

Article VIII. Hearsay

DEFINITIONS

The following definitions apply under this article:

(a) Statement. A "statement" is (1) an oral or written assertion or (2) nonverbal conduct of a person, if it is intended by the person as an assertion.

(b) Declarant. A "declarant" is a person who makes a statement.

(c) Hearsay. "Hearsay" is a statement, other than one made by the declarant while testifying at the trial or hearing, offered in evidence to prove the truth of the matter asserted.

(d) Statements Which Are Not Hearsay. A statement is not hearsay if -

> **(1) Prior Statement by Witness.** The declarant testifies at the trial or hearing and is subject to cross-examination concerning the statement, and the statement is (A) inconsistent with the declarant's testimony, or (B) consistent with the declarant's testimony and is offered to rebut an express or implied charge against the declarant of recent fabrication or improper influence or motive; provided, however, the statement must have been made before the alleged fabrication, or before the alleged improper influence or motive arose, or (C) one of identification of a person made after perceiving

the person, or (D) consistent with the declarant's testimony in a criminal sexual conduct case or attempted criminal sexual conduct case where the declarant is the alleged victim and the statement is limited to the time and place of the incident; or

(2) Admission by Party-Opponent. The statement is offered against a party and is (A) the party's own statement in either an individual or a representative capacity, or (B) a statement of which the party has manifested an adoption or belief in its truth, or (C) a statement by a person authorized by the party to make a statement concerning the subject, or (D) a statement by the party's agent or servant concerning a matter within the scope of the agency or employment, made during the existence of the relationship, or (E) a statement by a coconspirator of a party during the course and in furtherance of the conspiracy.

Note:

With the exception of subsection (d)(1), this rule is identical to the federal rule.

While case law has not defined the words "statement" and "declarant," the definitions in subsections (a) and (b) are consistent with how those words are used in numerous cases discussing the hearsay rule. Prior law recognized that wordless conduct intended as a communication may be hearsay. State v. Williams, 285 S.C. 544, 331 S.E.2d 354 (Ct. App. 1985).

Subsection (c) is consistent with South Carolina law. Player v. Thompson, 259 S.C. 600, 193 S.E.2d 531 (1972).

Subsection (d)(1) changes the law in South Carolina. Previously, where the declarant testified at trial and was subject to cross-examination, the general rule was that prior statements made by the declarant/witness were admissible regardless of the hearsay nature of the statements. See State v. Garner, 304 S.C. 220, 403 S.E.2d 631 (1991); State v. Caldwell, 283 S.C. 350, 322 S.E.2d 662 (1984); State v. Plyler, 275 S.C. 291, 270 S.E.2d 126 (1980); but see State v. Munn, 292 S.C. 497, 357 S.E.2d 461 (1987) (all out-of-court statements made by alleged victim not necessarily admissible simply because victim testifies at trial). Subsection (d)(1), however, treats prior statements of a witness as not being hearsay in only four instances. Subsection (A) omits the requirement of the federal rule that the declarant's prior inconsistent statement be given under oath. This modification renders the rule consistent with South Carolina law. See State v. Copeland, 278 S.C. 572, 300 S.E.2d 63 (1982), cert. denied, 460 U.S. 1103, 103 S.Ct. 1802, 76 L.Ed.2d 367 (1983). It should be noted that the foundation requirements of Rule 613(b) must be met before extrinsic evidence of a prior inconsistent statement is admissible. Subsection (B) is the federal rule modified by adding the phrase "provided, however, the statement must have been made before the alleged fabrication, or before the alleged improper influence or motive arose." This modification, which is taken from the United States Supreme Court's interpretation of Rule 801(d)(1)(B) of the Federal Rules of Evidence in Tome v. United States, 513 U.S. 150, 130 L.Ed.2d 574, 115 S.Ct. 696 (1995), is somewhat similar to the limitation previously contained in the case law that a prior consistent statement is admissible only where it was made prior to the declarant's relation to the cause. Jolly v. State, 314 S.C. 17, 443 S.E.2d 566 (1994); Burns v. Clayton, 237 S.C. 316, 117 S.E.2d 300 (1960). Subsection (C) is identical to the federal rule and consistent with South Carolina law that evidence regarding pre-trial identifications, which are not the product of

122

unconstitutional procedures, are admissible. State v. Stewart, 275 S.C. 447, 272 S.E.2d 628 (1980); State v. Gambrell, 274 S.C. 587, 266 S.E.2d 78 (1980). Subsection (D), which is not contained in the federal rule, was added to make admissible in criminal sexual conduct cases evidence that the victim complained of the sexual assault, limited to the time and place of the assault. Subsection (D) is consistent with South Carolina law. Jolly v. State, 314 S.C. 17, 443 S.E.2d 566 (1994).

Subsection (d)(2)(A) is consistent with South Carolina law. Bunch v. Cobb, 273 S.C. 445, 257 S.E.2d 225 (1979) (admission against interest of a party opponent is admissible); State v. Good, 308 S.C. 313, 417 S.E.2d 643 (Ct. App. 1992) (an out of court admission of a criminal defendant is admissible). Subsection (B) is consistent with South Carolina law. State v. Sharpe, 239 S.C. 258, 122 S.E.2d 622 (1962) (testimony that defendant was silent in response to an accusation by a third party admissible), rev'd on other grounds, State v. Torrence, 305 S.C. 45, 406 S.E.2d 315 (1991); Coleman & Lipscomb v. Frazier, 38 S.C.L. (4 Rich.) 146 (1850) (where party received a statement and acted on it as true, statement admissible). Subsection (C) is consistent with South Carolina law. Harper v. American Ry. Express Co., 139 S.C. 545, 138 S.E. 354 (1927) (statements by a person authorized to speak are admissible). Subsection (D) is consistent with South Carolina law that statements made by an agent in the scope of his authority were admissible. Hunter v. Hyder, 236 S.C. 378, 114 S.E.2d 493 (1960). Subsection (E) is consistent with South Carolina law. State v. Sullivan, 277 S.C. 35, 282 S.E.2d 838 (1981); Yeager v. Murphy, 291 S.C. 485, 354 S.E.2d 393 (Ct. App. 1987) (statements made by co-conspirators in furtherance of the conspiracy are admissible).

Explanation

What is hearsay? An out of court statement offered to prove the truth of the matter asserted.

What is not hearsay? There are five statements that are not considered hearsay:

- ❖ Prior inconsistent statement: a witness can be impeached by a prior inconsistent statement they gave. This rule differs from the Federal Rule in that the prior statement does not have to be sworn.

- ❖ Prior consistent statement: Generally you cannot bolster a witness's credibility by showing that they previously said the same thing at an earlier date. However, if the declarant is accused of recently changing their story (e.g. they were bribed to testify today), then you can introduce evidence of a prior statement that shows they have been saying the same thing before the alleged bribery.

- ❖ Prior identification of a person after perceiving that person

- ❖ Statement by CSC victim about time and place of incident (victim is testifying)

- ❖ Admission by party opponent: In a criminal case, generally anything the defendant has said is not hearsay. In a civil case, generally anything the plaintiff or defendant has said is not hearsay. This also includes any statements by a coconspirator of the defendant during the conspiracy and in furtherance of the conspiracy. Remember, the statement is not hearsay if it is used against the other party.

Case Law

"Appellant specifically challenges the portions of the report where the mother related to Williams that the middle child told her appellant molested her and specific things the victims told the forensic interviewer during the interviews. We find these portions of the written reports constitute inadmissible hearsay as they were out-of-court statements offered to prove that appellant did in fact inappropriately touch the girls in the way that they claimed."
State v. Jennings, 394 S.C. 473, 479 (2011).

Prior inconsistent statement

"A prior inconsistent statement may be admitted as substantive evidence when the declarant testifies at trial and is subject to cross-examination."
State v. Stokes, 381 S.C. 390, 398–99, 673 S.E.2d 434, 438 (2009)

"Heretofore, South Carolina has followed the traditional rule that testimony of inconsistent statements is admissible only to impeach the credibility of the witness. Henceforth from today, we will allow testimony of prior inconsistent statements to be used as substantive evidence when the declarant testifies at trial and is subject to cross examination."
State v. Copeland, 278 S.C. 572, 581, 300 S.E.2d 63, 69 (1982)

Prior consistent statement

"Likewise, in the instant case, Michelle's statement was inadmissible because there was no express or implied charge against Michelle of recent fabrication or improper influence or motive. Foster's questions did not rise to the level of charging fabrication, but instead amounted to calling her

credibility into question, i.e., simple impeachment.[5] Thus, because the requirements of Rule 801(d)(1)(B) were not met in the instant case, the written consistent statement was inadmissible hearsay, and the trial court erred in allowing the statement. *Id.* This error served only to **improperly** bolster Michelle's testimony. *See Tome v. United States,* 513 U.S. 150, 157–58, 115 S.Ct. 696, 130 L.Ed.2d 574 (1995) (discussing federal[6] Rule 801(d)(1)(B) and stating that the purpose of the rule is to rebut an alleged fabrication or motive, not to 'bolster[ ] the veracity of the story told.')."
State v. Foster, 354 S.C. 614, 622–23, 582 S.E.2d 426, 430 (2003)

Admission: conspiracy

"Rule 801(d)(2)(E) provides that a statement by a co-conspirator during the course and in furtherance of the conspiracy is not hearsay. Under the Federal Rules of Evidence, this same rule has been interpreted to allow admission of a co-conspirator's statement only where there is evidence of the conspiracy *independent* of the statement sought to be admitted. Here, there is no independent evidence of a conspiracy between Robertson and appellant. The fact that Robertson was *indicted* for criminal conspiracy is not sufficient in itself to establish a conspiracy since an indictment is not evidence of the crime charged."
State v. Gilchrist, 342 S.C. 369, 372, 536 S.E.2d 868, 869 (2000) (citations omitted)

Legal documents

"Written contracts 'offered in court not for the truth of any facts stated in [them] but to prove the existence of a contractual right or duty' should not be excluded as hearsay. *Kepner–Tregoe, Inc. v. Leadership Software, Inc.* (Signed instruments such as wills, contracts, and promissory notes are

writings that have independent legal significance, and are non [-]hearsay.).""
Deep Keel, LLC v. Atl. Private Equity Grp., LLC, 413 S.C. 58, 70, 773 S.E.2d 607, 613 (Ct. App. 2015) (citation omitted)

"However, the master's reliance on a hearsay exception was unnecessary because the loan documents were not hearsay in the first place. The loan documents form the basis of Deep Keel's claim that Community First loaned Atlantic money in exchange for an obligation to pay it back and a security interest in the real estate. Thus, the loan documents were offered to establish the existence of a contract and the terms of that contract. Written contracts 'offered in court not for the truth of any facts stated in [them] but to prove the existence of a contractual right or duty' should not be excluded as hearsay. 31A C.J.S. *Evidence* § 462 (2008); *see also Kepner–Tregoe, Inc. v. Leadership Software, Inc.,* 12 F.3d 527, 540 (5th Cir.1994) ('Signed instruments such as wills, contracts, and promissory notes are writings that have independent legal significance, and are non [-]hearsay.'); *Fields v. J. Haynes Waters Builders, Inc.,* 376 S.C. 545, 559, 658 S.E.2d 80, 87 (2008) (recognizing that 'words of contract' are non-hearsay when they are not 'offered for the truth of the matter asserted' and 'form[ ] part of an issue' being litigated). We find the loan documents were properly admitted to show the existence of an agreement to loan money, the terms of repayment, and the existence of a security interest in the real estate. Because the loan documents were not offered to prove the truth of any statement, they were not hearsay and the master correctly admitted them."
Deep Keel, LLC v. Atl. Private Equity Grp., LLC, 413 S.C. 58, 69–70, 773 S.E.2d 607, 613 (Ct. App. 2015)

RULE 802
HEARSAY RULE

Hearsay is not admissible except as provided by these rules or by other rules prescribed by the Supreme Court of this State or by statute.

Note:

The rule replaces the words "by the Supreme Court pursuant to statutory authority or by Act of Congress" found in the federal rule with "by the Supreme Court of this State or by statute." It is consistent with the general rule that hearsay is not admissible unless it fits within an exception to the hearsay rule. Jolly v. State, 314 S.C. 17, 443 S.E.2d 566 (1994); Lee v. Gulf Ins. Co., 248 S.C. 296, 149 S.E.2d 639 (1966).

Case Law

"The Hearsay Rule provides that '[h]earsay is not admissible except as provided by these rules or by other rules prescribed by the Supreme Court of this State or by statute.' Rule 802, SCRE."
State v. Kromah, 401 S.C. 340, 355, 737 S.E.2d 490, 498 (2013)

RULE 803
HEARSAY EXCEPTIONS; AVAILABILITY OF DECLARANT IMMATERIAL

The following are not excluded by the hearsay rule, even though the declarant is available as a witness:

(1) Present Sense Impression. A statement describing or explaining an event or condition made while the declarant was perceiving the event or condition, or immediately thereafter.

(2) Excited Utterance. A statement relating to a startling event or condition made while the declarant was under the stress of excitement caused by the event or condition.

(3) Then Existing Mental, Emotional, or Physical Condition. A statement of the declarant's then existing state of mind, emotion, sensation, or physical condition (such as intent, plan, motive, design, mental feeling, pain, and bodily health), but not including a statement of memory or belief to prove the fact remembered or believed unless it relates to the execution, revocation, identification, or terms of declarant's will.

(4) Statements for Purposes of Medical Diagnosis or Treatment. Statements made for purposes of medical diagnosis or treatment and describing medical history, or past or present symptoms, pain, or sensations, or the inception or general character of the cause or external source thereof insofar as reasonably pertinent to diagnosis or treatment; provided, however, that the admissibility of statements made after commencement of the litigation is left to the court's discretion.

(5) Recorded Recollection. A memorandum or record concerning a matter about which a witness once had knowledge but now has insufficient recollection to enable the witness to testify fully and accurately, shown to have been made or adopted by the witness when the matter was fresh in the witness' memory and to reflect that knowledge correctly. If admitted, the memorandum or record may be read into evidence but may not itself be received as an exhibit unless offered by an adverse party.

(6) Records of Regularly Conducted Activity. A memorandum, report, record, or data compilation, in any form, of acts, events, conditions, or diagnoses, made at or near the time by, or from information transmitted by, a person with knowledge, if kept in the course of a regularly conducted business activity, and if it was the regular practice of that business activity to make the memorandum, report, record, or data compilation, all as shown by the testimony of the custodian or other qualified witness, unless the source of information or the method or circumstances of preparation indicate lack of trustworthiness; provided, however, that subjective opinions and judgments found in business records are not admissible. The term "business" as used in this subsection includes business, institution, association, profession, occupation, and calling of every kind, whether or not conducted for profit.

(7) Absence of Entry in Records Kept in Accordance With the Provisions of Subsection (6). Evidence that a matter is not included in the memoranda, reports, records, or data compilations, in any form, kept in accordance with the provisions of subsection (6), to prove the nonoccurrence or nonexistence of the matter, if the matter was of a kind of which a memorandum, report, record, or data compilation was regularly made and preserved, unless the sources of information or other circumstances indicate lack of trustworthiness.

(8) Public Records and Reports. Records, reports, statements, or data compilations, in any form, of public offices or agencies, setting forth (A) the activities of the office or agency, or (B) matters observed pursuant to duty imposed by law as to which matters there was a duty to report, excluding, however, in criminal cases matters observed by police officers and other law enforcement personnel; provided, however, that investigative notes involving opinions, judgments, or conclusions are not admissible. Accident reports required by S.C. Code Ann. §§ 56-5-1260 to -1280 (1991) are not admissible as evidence of negligence or due care in an action at law for damages.

(9) Records of Vital Statistics. Records or data compilations, in any form, of births, fetal deaths, deaths, or marriages, if the report thereof was made to a public office pursuant to requirements of law.

(10) Absence of Public Record or Entry. To prove the absence of a record, report, statement, or data compilation, in any form, or the nonoccurrence or nonexistence of a matter of which a record, report, statement or data compilation, in any form, was regularly made and preserved by a public office or agency, evidence in the form of a certification in accordance with Rule 902, or testimony, that diligent search failed to disclose the record, report, statement, or data compilation, or entry.

(11) Records of Religious Organizations. Statements of births, marriages, divorces, deaths, legitimacy, ancestry, relationship by blood or marriage, or other similar facts of personal or family history, contained in a regularly kept record of a religious organization.

(12) Marriage, Baptismal, and Similar Certificates. Statements of fact contained in a certificate that the maker performed a marriage or other ceremony or administered a sacrament, made by a clergyman, public official, or other person authorized by the rules or practices of a religious organization or by law to perform the act certified, and purporting to have been issued at the time of the act or within a reasonable time thereafter.

(13) Family Records. Statements of fact concerning personal or family history contained in family Bibles, genealogies, charts, engravings on rings, inscriptions on family portraits, engravings on urns, crypts, or tombstones, or the like.

(14) Records of Documents Affecting an Interest in Property. The record of a document purporting to establish or affect an interest in property, as proof of the content of the original recorded document and its execution and delivery by each person by whom it purports to have been executed, if the record is a record of a public office and an applicable statute authorizes the recording of documents of that kind in that office.

(15) Statements in Documents Affecting an Interest in Property. A statement contained in a document purporting to establish or affect an interest in property if the matter stated was relevant to the purpose of the document, unless dealings with the property since the document was made have been inconsistent with the truth of the statement or the purport of the document.

(16) Statements in Ancient Documents. Statements in a document in existence twenty years or more the authenticity of which is established.

(17) Market Reports, Commercial Publications. Market quotations, tabulations, lists, directories, or other published compilations, generally used and relied upon by the public or by persons in particular occupations.

(18) Learned Treatises. To the extent called to the attention of an expert witness upon cross-examination or relied upon by the expert witness in direct examination, statements contained in published treatises, periodicals, or pamphlets on a subject of history, medicine, or other science or art, established as a reliable authority by the testimony or admission of the witness or by other expert testimony or by judicial notice. If admitted, the statements may be read into evidence but may not be received as exhibits. This rule is in addition to any statutory provisions on this subject.

(19) Reputation Concerning Personal or Family History. Reputation among members of a person's family by blood, adoption, or marriage, or among a person's associates, or in the community, concerning a person's birth, adoption, marriage, divorce, death, legitimacy, relationship by blood, adoption, or marriage, ancestry, or other similar fact of personal or family history.

(20) Reputation Concerning Boundaries or General History. Reputation in a community, arising before the controversy, as to boundaries of or customs affecting lands in the community, and reputation as to events of general history important to the community or State or nation in which located.

(21) Reputation as to Character. Reputation of a person's character among associates or in the community.

(22) Judgment of Previous Conviction. Evidence of a final judgment (to include final judgments in juvenile delinquency matters), entered after a trial or upon a plea of guilty (but not upon a plea of nolo contendere), adjudging a person guilty of a crime punishable by death or imprisonment in excess of one year, to prove any fact essential to sustain the judgment, but not including, when offered by the Government in a criminal prosecution for purposes other than impeachment, judgments against persons other than the accused. The pendency of an appeal may be shown but does not affect admissibility.

(23) Judgment as to Personal, Family or General History, or Boundaries. Judgments as proof of matters of personal, family or general history, or boundaries, essential to the judgment, if the same would be provable by evidence of reputation.

Note:

Except for modifications to subsections (4), (6), (8), (18), and (22), and the deletion of subsection (24) which contained a "catchall" or residual hearsay exception, this rule is identical to the federal rule.

Subsections (1) and (2): These subsections constitute a change in South Carolina law. Previously, a statement had to meet the conditions of both subsections (1) and (2) before it would be admissible under the res gestae exception to the hearsay rule. State v. Harrison, 298 S.C. 333, 380 S.E.2d 818 (1989).

Subsection (3): This subsection is consistent with prior state practice. Winburn v. Minnesota Mut. Life Ins. Co., 261 S.C. 568, 201 S.E.2d 372 (1973); Sligh v. Newberry Elec.Coop.,Inc., 216 S.C. 401, 58 S.E.2d 675 (1950); Ervin v. Myrtle Grove Plantation, 206 S.C. 41, 32 S.E.2d 877 (1945); Lazar v. Great Atl.& Pac. Tea Co., 197 S.C. 74, 14 S.E.2d 560 (1941); Spires v. Spires, 111 S.C. 373, 97 S.E. 847 (1919).

Subsection (4): The first part of this subsection is identical to the federal rule and is consistent with state practice. State v. Camele, 293 S.C. 302, 360 S.E.2d 307 (1987) (physician's testimony should include only those statements related to him by the patient upon which the physician relied in reaching medical conclusions); Gentry v. Watkins-Carolina Trucking Co., 249 S.C. 316, 154 S.E.2d 112 (1967) (statements of present condition and past symptoms made to a physician consulted as a potential witness are admissible, not as substantive evidence, but, in the absence of fraud or bad faith, as information upon which the physician relied in reaching a professional opinion). The final phrase was added to the subsection to provide that the admissibility of statements made after commencement of the litigation is within the trial judge's discretion. Gentry v. Watkins-Carolina Trucking Co., supra.

Subsection (5): This subsection is similar to previous state law which allowed a witness to testify from a writing when it was the original document prepared by the witness contemporaneously with the event for the purpose of preserving the memory of it. Gwathmey v. Foor Hotel Co., 121 S.C. 237, 113 S.E. 688 (1922); The Bank of Charleston Nat'l Banking Ass'n v. Zorn, 14 S.C. 444 (1881). The provision of this rule limiting the introduction of the writing to when it is offered by an adverse party is a change in South Carolina law.

135

Subsection (6): This subsection differs from the federal rule in that the word "opinions" in the first sentence is deleted and the phrase, "provided, however, that subjective opinions and judgments found in business records are not admissible" is added to the federal rule to make it consistent with state law. Kershaw County Dep't of Social Serv. v. McCaskill, 276 S.C. 360, 278 S.E.2d 771 (1981); see also State v. Rich, 293 S.C. 172, 359 S.E.2d 281 (1987) (admission of properly authenticated fingerprints); Uniform Business Records as Evidence Act, S.C. Code Ann. § 19-5-510 (1985).

Subsection (7): While the case law has recognized the admissibility of negative evidence to prove the non-existence of records of regularly conducted activity, the courts have not recognized this as a separate hearsay exception. E.g., Peoples Nat'l Bank v. Manos Bros., Inc., 226 S.C. 257, 84 S.E.2d 857 (1955); see also Flowers v. South Carolina Dep't of Highways and Pub. Transp., 309 S.C. 76, 419 S.E.2d 832 (Ct. App. 1992) (citing federal rule).

Subsection (8): This subsection differs from the federal rule in that it does not include item (C). The subsection also contains two limitations not included in the federal rule. First, investigative notes involving opinions, judgments, or conclusions are not admissible. Further, accident reports required by statute are not admissible as evidence of negligence or due care in actions for damages. As modified, this subsection is consistent with prior state practice. State v. Pearson, 223 S.C. 377, 76 S.E.2d 151 (1953); S.C. Code Ann. § 56-5-1290 (1991); see also State v. Rich, 293 S.C. 172, 359 S.E.2d 281 (1987) (admission of properly authenticated fingerprints).

Subsection (9): This subsection constitutes a change in South Carolina law. Prior case law limited admissions of such reports to matters within the knowledge of the person making the report. Williams v. Metropolitan Life Ins. Co., 116 S.C. 277, 108 S.E. 110 (1921).

Subsection (10): While the case law has recognized the admissibility of negative evidence to prove the non-existence of public records, the courts have not recognized this as a separate hearsay exception. See Peoples Nat'l Bank v. Manos Bros., Inc., 226 S.C. 257, 84 S.E.2d 857 (1955) (introduction of evidence of the non-existence of public record entries); Flowers v. South Carolina Dep't of Highways and Pub. Transp., 309 S.C. 76, 419 S.E.2d 832 (Ct.App.1992) (citing federal rule). See also Rule 44(b), SCRCP.

Subsection (11): There does not appear to be any South Carolina law concerning this exception to the hearsay rule.

Subsection (12): No prior South Carolina authority has been found which states the hearsay exception expressed in this subsection.

Subsection (13): This exception is apparently consistent with prior case law in this State. See Dobson v. Cothran, 34 S.C. 518, 13 S.E. 679 (1891) (entry in family Bible of the birth date of a person is admissible as evidence of the person's age only where better evidence cannot be obtained).

Subsection (14): This subsection is consistent with statutory and case law in this State. Wilson v. Moseley, 113 S.C. 278, 102 S.E. 330 (1920) (a record book from a clerk's office, wherein a deed was authorized to be recorded and was recorded, is admissible to prove the existence and contents of the deed if sufficient evidence is presented to prove that the original deed is not available); S.C. Code Ann. § 19-5-10

(1985) (admissibility of certified copies or certified photostatic copies of documents).

Subsection (15): This provision is apparently consistent with prior case law in this State. See Smith v. Williams, 141 S.C. 265, 139 S.E. 625 (1927) (husband's statements in a deed and accompanying memorandum purporting to convey an interest in property admissible to show whether family agreement had been made following husband's death entitling widow to retain use and possession of the property).

Subsection (16): The ancient document exception to the hearsay rule in subsection (16) is consistent with prior case law in this State. However, prior case law qualified a document as "ancient" if the document was thirty years old or older. Atlantic Coast Line R.R. Co. v. Searson, 137 S.C. 468, 135 S.E. 567 (1926) (map more than thirty years old could be introduced as ancient document); Johnson v. Pritchard, 302 S.C. 437, 395 S.E.2d 191 (Ct. App. 1990) (duly authenticated ancient documents of thirty years or more constitute an exception to the hearsay rule). Subsection (16) qualifies a document as "ancient" if it is twenty years old or older.

Subsection (17): This provision is consistent with prior case law in this State. Peoples Nat'l Bank v. Manos Bros., Inc., 226 S.C. 257, 84 S.E.2d 857 (1954) (on the issue of domicile, a city directory is admissible); Kirkpatrick v. Hardeman, 123 S.C. 21, 115 S.E. 905 (1923) (accredited current price lists and market reports, including those published in trade journals or newspapers, which are accepted as trustworthy, are admissible on the question of market value of stock).

Subsection (18): This exception is identical to the federal rule except for the addition of the last sentence. This rule changes and expands previous South Carolina law which held that

138

medical books are not admissible into evidence to be read to the court and jury except in the situations set forth in S.C. Code Ann. § 19-5-410 (1985). See LaCount v. General Asbestos & Rubber Co., 184 S.C. 232, 192 S.E. 262 (1937); Baker v. Southern Cotton Oil Co., 161 S.C. 479, 159 S.E. 822 (1931); Edwards v. Union Buffalo Mills Co., 162 S.C. 17, 159 S.E. 818 (1931). This rule is consistent with the case of Baker v. Port City Steel Erectors, Inc., 261 S.C. 469, 200 S.E.2d 681 (1973), which states that a scientific textbook can be used for the purpose of impeaching an expert witness.

Subsection (19): This exception is consistent with prior state law. Hazelwood v. Mayes, 111 S.C. 23, 96 S.E. 672 (1918); Horry v. Glover, 11 S.C.Eq. (2 Hill Eq.) 515 (1837).

Subsection (20): This exception is consistent with prior state law. Culbertson v. Culbertson, 273 S.C. 103, 254 S.E.2d 558 (1979) (boundary); County of Darlington v. Perkins, 269 S.C. 572, 239 S.E.2d 69 (1977) (general history).

Subsection (21): There is no South Carolina law dealing with this exception. This section is included in the rules to insure that reputation evidence is not excluded on the basis of hearsay. See Weinstein's Evidence ¶ 803(21)[01] (1994). Rules 404, 405, and 608 deal with when reputation evidence may be admissible.

Subsection (22): This subsection is identical to the federal rule except for the addition of the phrase "to include final judgments in juvenile delinquency matters." This addition makes it clear that a final judgment in a juvenile delinquency matter is to be treated in the same manner as an adult conviction under this subsection; to determine if the crime is punishable by death or imprisonment in excess of one year, the maximum punishment an adult would receive for the

139

offense is controlling. Traditionally, evidence of a judgment in a criminal case was not admissible in a civil case as evidence of the facts upon which the conviction was based. <u>Fontville v. Atlanta & Charlotte Air Line Ry. Co.</u>, 93 S.C. 287, 75 S.E. 172 (1910). This traditional rule has, however, been eroded in several cases. <u>South Carolina State Board of Dental Examiners v. Breeland</u>, 208 S.C. 469, 38 S.E.2d 644 (1946) (at least where the police power of the state is involved in a civil case, a criminal conviction based on a jury verdict is admissible); <u>Globe & Rutgers Fire Ins. Co. v. Foil</u>, 189 S.C. 91, 200 S.E. 97 (1938) (evidence of a conviction based on a guilty plea is admissible in a civil case as an admission against the criminal defendant). The adoption of this rule now allows criminal judgments based on a plea of guilty or a trial for an offense which carries a maximum punishment of death or imprisonment for more than one year to be admissible in almost all civil actions to prove the facts essential to the criminal judgment. Not allowing a criminal judgment based on a plea of nolo contendere to be used to prove the facts on which the judgment is based is consistent with the prior case law. <u>Kibler v. State</u>, 267 S.C. 250, 227 S.E.2d 199 (1976) (plea of nolo cannot be used as an admission in a civil case); <u>see also</u> <u>In re Anderson</u>, 255 S.C. 56, 177 S.E.2d 130 (1970) (attorney disciplinary proceeding). It should be noted that S.C. Code Ann. § 56-5-6160 (1991) limits the admissibility of evidence of a conviction for a traffic offense. Further, S.C. Code Ann. § 20-7-780 (Supp. 1993), which makes juvenile records confidential unless otherwise ordered by the family court, may limit access to final judgments in juvenile delinquency matters.

Subsection (23): This exception is consistent with prior state law. <u>Bradley v. Calhoun</u>, 116 S.C. 7, 106 S.E. 843 (1921).

Explanation

Even if it is hearsay, we will still let it in if it falls under one of these 23 exceptions. These 23 different types of hearsay are so reliable, that the court does not need the person who actually said it to be at trial to testify.

Take note: *Crawford* and the confrontation clause usually arise when a hearsay statement is being discussed. *Crawford* applies to statements that are A.) Offered for its truth and B.) Testimonial. If the statement checks both of those, then the declarant of that statement has to either A.) Testify at trial or B.) Unavailable and had a prior opportunity to be cross examined.

Crawford is a constitutional issue and must be ruled on before deciding any rules of evidence issues.

Case Law

Crawford

"The United States Supreme Court has held the Confrontation Clause prohibits the admission of out-of-court testimonial statements of a witness unless the witness is unavailable to testify and the defendant had a prior opportunity to cross-examine the witness. The *Crawford* Court stated the 'core class of testimonial statements' includes: (1) ex parte in-court testimony or its functional equivalent, (2) extrajudicial statements contained in formalized testimonial materials, (3) statements made under circumstances that would lead an objective witness to reasonably believe that the statement would be available for use at a later trial, and (4) statements taken by police officers in the course of interrogations. However, the Court noted the Confrontation Clause 'does not bar the use of testimonial statements for purposes other than establishing the truth of the matter asserted.' Accordingly, 'an out of court statement is not hearsay if it is offered for the limited purpose of explaining why a government investigation was undertaken.' "

State v. Davis, 420 S.C. 50, 67 (Ct. App. 2017) (citations omitted)

"Finally, in *Crawford v. Washington*, 541 U.S. 36, 54, 124 S.Ct. 1354, 158 L.Ed.2d 177 (2004), the United States Supreme Court noted the hearsay exception for business records and observed that business records are not 'testimonial' and therefore do not implicate the Confrontation Clause. A public record, very much like a business record, is not testimonial and its admission similarly does not violate the defendant's confrontation rights. Moreover, appellant was able to cross-examine Dr. Ophoven regarding the possible inaccuracies in these autopsy reports and presented extensive expert testimony reinterpreting the significance of their findings.[7] We find appellant's confrontation rights were not infringed."
State v. Cutro, 365 S.C. 366, 378, 618 S.E.2d 890, 896 (2005)

Testimonial

"Whatever else the term covers, it applies at a minimum to prior testimony at a preliminary hearing, before a grand jury, or at a former trial; and to police interrogations."
Crawford v. Washington, 541 U.S. 36, 68 (2004)

"Under the primary purpose analysis required by the Confrontation Clause, where the primary purpose of an out-of-court statement is to serve as evidence or 'an out-of-court substitute for trial testimony,' the statement is considered testimonial."
State v. Brockmeyer, 406 S.C. 324, 342 (2013)

Present Sense Impression

"There are three elements to the foundation for the admission of a hearsay statement as a present sense impression: (1) the statement must describe or explain an event or condition; (2) the statement must be contemporaneous with the event; and (3) the declarant must have personally perceived the event." State v. Hendricks, 408 S.C. 525, 533, 759 S.E.2d 434, 438 (Ct. App. 2014)

"In this case, the testimony of the nurse and the police officer is not admissible as a present sense impression. The victim gave her story to the officer at approximately 10:30 p.m., and she did not report to the hospital until approximately 11:00 p.m., nearly ten hours after the incident. Given this lapse of time, it cannot be said that the victim made the statements while she was 'perceiving the event or condition, or immediately thereafter,' as required by Rule 803(1)." State v. Burroughs, 328 S.C. 489, 499 (Ct. App. 1997)

Excited Utterance

"Three elements must be met in order for a statement to be an excited utterance: (1) the statement must relate to a startling event or condition; (2) the statement must have been made while the declarant was under the stress of excitement; and (3) the stress of excitement must be caused by the startling event or condition. *State v. Ladner,* 373 S.C. 103, 116, 644 S.E.2d 684, 691 (2007). The rationale underlying the excited utterance exception is that 'the startling event suspends the declarant's process of reflective thought, reducing the likelihood of fabrication.' *State v. Davis,* 371 S.C. 170, 178, 638 S.E.2d 57, 62 (2006). A court must consider the totality of the circumstances when determining whether a statement is admissible under the excited utterance exception, and the

determination is generally left to the sound discretion of the trial court."
State v. Washington, 379 S.C. 120, 124, 665 S.E.2d 602, 604 (2008)

"The rationale underlying the excited utterance exception is that 'the startling event suspends the declarant's process of reflective thought, reducing the likelihood of fabrication.' A court must consider the totality of the circumstances when determining whether a statement falls within the excited utterance exception. Nonetheless, 'the burden of establishing the facts which qualify a statement as an excited utterance rests with the proponent of the evidence.' ('The party offering the statement as an exception to the rule against hearsay has the burden of making a sufficient showing of spontaneity to render the statement admissible.'). Finally, statements which are not based on firsthand information, such as where the declarant was not an actual witness to the event, are not admissible under the excited utterance exception to the hearsay rule."
State v. Davis, 371 S.C. 170, 178–79 (2006) (citations omitted)

State of Mind

"Like Rule 803(3), FRE, Rule 803(3), SCRE, 'does not permit a statement of memory or belief to prove the fact remembered,' unless relating to the declarant's will. *Id.* The purpose of this exclusion is 'to avoid the virtual destruction of the hearsay rule which would otherwise result from allowing state of mind, provable by a hearsay statement, to serve as a basis for an inference of the happening of the event which produced the state of mind.'[3] Advisory Committee Note to Rule 803(3), FRE. Consequently, while the present state of the declarant's mind is admissible as an exception to hearsay, the reason for the declarant's state of mind is

not. *United States v. Cohen,* 631 F.2d 1223, 1225 (5th Cir.1980) ('But the state-of-mind exception does not permit the witness to relate any of the declarant's statements as to why he held the particular state of mind, or what he might have believed that would have induced the state of mind. If the reservation in the text of the rule is to have any effect, it must be understood to narrowly limit those admissible statements to declarations of condition—'I'm scared'—and not belief—'I'm scared because [someone] threatened me'.')."
State v. Garcia, 334 S.C. 71, 76, 512 S.E.2d 507, 509 (1999)

"We find these statements were inadmissible because they not only revealed Jeanine's fearful state of mind, they described the reason for it. ('[W]hile the present state of the declarant's mind is admissible as an exception to hearsay, the reason for the declarant's state of mind is not.')."
State v. Daise, 421 S.C. 442, 460 (Ct. App. 2017) (citations omitted)

Medical diagnosis

"This hearsay exception requires that the statements be provided for the purpose of and be reasonably pertinent to medical diagnosis or   treatment. Rule 803(4),   SCRE. Rule 803(4), SCRE, may well apply in a CSC case, but there must be a nexus between the information provided by the patient and the diagnosis or treatment of the patient. For example, after recent trauma, these type of statements can provide the doctor with specific areas to focus on or specific conditions to search for when performing the diagnostic physical exam and are reasonably pertinent to diagnosis or treatment. In this regard, 'a statement that the victim had been raped or that the assailant had hurt the victim in a particular area would be pertinent to the diagnosis and treatment of the victim.' *State v. Burroughs,* 328 S.C. 489, 501, 492 S.E.2d

145

408, 414 (Ct. App. 1997). However, '[a] doctor's testimony as to history should include only those facts related to him by the victim upon which he relied in reaching his medical conclusions. The doctor's testimony should never be used as a tool to prove facts properly proved by other witnesses.' *State v. Brown*, 286 S.C. 445, 447, 334 S.E.2d 816, 817 (1985); *see also* Rule 803(4), SCRE, Note (stating a 'physician's testimony should include only those statements related to him by the patient upon which the physician relied in reaching medical conclusions' (citing *State v. Camele*, 293 S.C. 302, 360 S.E.2d 307 (1987))."
State v. Simmons, 423 S.C. 552, 563–64, 816 S.E.2d 566, 572–73 (2018), reh'g denied (Aug. 2, 2018)

Business records

"Rule 803(6), SCRE, provides that memorandum, reports, records, etc. in any form, of acts, events, conditions, or diagnoses, are admissible as longs as they are (1) prepared near the time of the event recorded; (2) prepared by someone with or from information transmitted by a person with knowledge; (3) prepared in the regular course of business; (4) identified by a qualified witness who can testify regarding the mode of preparation of the record; and (5) found to be trustworthy by the court. Rule 803(6), SCRE; S.C.Code Ann. § 19-5-510 (Supp.2001). Medical records are admitted routinely as business records."
Ex parte Dep't of Health & Envtl. Control, 350 S.C. 243, 249–50, 565 S.E.2d 293, 297 (2002)

Public records/Records of vital statistics

"Further, autopsy reports are not hearsay under Rule 803, SCRE. Subsection (8) of this rule excepts from hearsay public records and reports containing matters there is a duty to report. Autopsies are required in cases of SIDS if law enforcement

deems it necessary. S.C.Code Ann. § 17–5–540 (2003) and § 20–7–5915 (Supp.2004). Additionally, subsection (9) of Rule 803 specifically exempts from hearsay records of vital statistics, including 'reports ... of ... deaths ... if the report thereof was made to a public office pursuant to requirements of law.' Autopsy reports are required to be kept by the medical examiner's office. S.C.Code Ann. § 17–5–280 (2003). Accordingly, an autopsy report is not inadmissible hearsay."
State v. Cutro, 365 S.C. 366, 377–78, 618 S.E.2d 890, 896 (2005)

"Properly authenticated fingerprints are admissible against a criminal defendant. Further, under the business records exception or the public records exception, admission of police fingerprint records is generally considered not to violate the prohibition against hearsay. *Id. See* S.C.Code Ann. § 19–5–510 (1985) (Providing in regard to business records as evidence, '[a] record of an act, condition or event shall, insofar as relevant, be competent evidence if the custodian or other qualified witness testifies to its identity and the mode of its preparation, and if it was made in the regular course of business, at or near the time of the act, condition or event and if, in the opinion of the court, the sources of information, method and time of preparation were such as to justify its admission.'); Rule 803(8), SCRE (Providing in regard to public records and reports, '[r]ecords, reports, statements, or data compilations, in any form, of public offices or agencies, setting forth (A) the activities of the office or agency, or (B) matters observed pursuant to duty imposed by law as to which matters there was a duty to report ...' are not excluded by the hearsay rule.). However, the party offering fingerprints into evidence must comply with the usual requirements of authentication."
State v. Anderson, 378 S.C. 243, 247–48, 662 S.E.2d 461, 463 (Ct. App. 2008), aff'd, 386 S.C. 120, 687 S.E.2d 35 (2009) (citation omitted)

RULE 804

HEARSAY EXCEPTIONS; DECLARANT UNAVAILABLE

(a) Definition of Unavailability. "Unavailability as a witness" includes situations in which the declarant –

> **(1)** is exempted by ruling of the court on the ground of privilege from testifying concerning the subject matter of the declarant's statement; or
>
> **(2)** persists in refusing to testify concerning the subject matter of the declarant's statement despite an order of the court to do so; or
>
> **(3)** testifies to a lack of memory of the subject matter of the declarant's statement; or
>
> **(4)** is unable to be present or to testify at the hearing because of death or then existing physical or mental illness or infirmity; or
>
> **(5)** is absent from the hearing and the proponent of a statement has been unable to procure the declarant's attendance (or in the case of a hearsay exception under subdivision (b)(2), (3), or (4), the declarant's attendance or testimony) by process or other reasonable means.

A declarant is not unavailable as a witness if exemption, refusal, claim of lack of memory, inability, or absence is due to the procurement or wrongdoing of the proponent of a statement for the purpose of preventing the witness from attending or testifying.

(b) Hearsay Exceptions. The following are not excluded by the hearsay rule if the declarant is unavailable as a witness:

(1) Former Testimony. Testimony given as a witness at another hearing of the same or a different proceeding, or in a deposition taken in compliance with law in the course of the same or another proceeding, if the party against whom the testimony is now offered, or, in a civil action or proceeding, a predecessor in interest, had an opportunity and similar motive to develop the testimony by direct, cross, or redirect examination.

(2) Statement Under Belief of Impending Death. In a prosecution for homicide or in a civil action or proceeding, a statement made by a declarant while believing that the declarant's death was imminent, concerning the cause or circumstances of what the declarant believed to be impending death.

(3) Statement Against Interest. A statement which was at the time of its making so far contrary to the declarant's pecuniary or proprietary interest, or so far tended to subject the declarant to civil or criminal liability, or to render invalid a claim by the declarant against another, that a reasonable person in the declarant's position would not have made the statement unless believing it to be true. A statement tending to expose the declarant to criminal liability and offered to exculpate the accused is not admissible unless corroborating circumstances clearly indicate the trustworthiness of the statement.

(4) Statement of Personal or Family History. (A) A statement concerning the declarant's own birth, adoption, marriage, divorce, legitimacy, relationship by blood, adoption, or marriage, ancestry, or other similar fact of personal or family history, even though declarant had no means of acquiring personal knowledge of the matter stated; or (B) a statement concerning the foregoing matters, and death also, of another person, if the declarant was related to the other by blood, adoption, or marriage or was so intimately associated with the other's family as to be likely to have accurate information concerning the matter declared.

Note:

Subsection (a) is identical to the federal rule and consistent with South Carolina law. Riddle v. State, 314 S.C. 1, 443 S.E.2d 557 (1994) (witness unavailable who refuses to testify even after being threatened with contempt); State v. Doctor, 306 S.C. 527, 413 S.E.2d 36 (1992) (witness who asserts a privilege is unavailable); State v. Steadman, 216 S.C. 579, 59 S.E.2d 168, cert. denied, 340 U.S. 850, 71 S.Ct. 78, 95 L.Ed. 623 (1950) (witness who is absent from the jurisdiction and cannot be found is unavailable); State v. Rogers, 101 S.C. 280, 85 S.E. 636 (1914) (witness who is dead, insane, beyond the seas, or kept away by the contrivance of the opposing party is unavailable).

Subsection (b) omits subsection (5), the "catch all" or residual hearsay exception found in the federal rule, but is otherwise identical to the federal rule. Subsection (1) is consistent with South Carolina law. State v. Steadman, 216 S.C. 579, 59 S.E.2d 168, cert. denied, 340 U.S. 850, 71 S.Ct. 78, 95 L.Ed. 623 (1950). It should be noted that S.C. Code Ann. § 19-11-50 (1985), which provides that the testimony of a criminal defendant may not be used in any subsequent criminal case against him except prosecution for perjury founded on that testimony, may place some limit on the admissibility of evidence under this subsection. Subsection (2) broadens the admissibility of dying declarations by making them admissible in civil cases. See Sligh v. Newberry Electric Co-op., 216 S.C. 401, 58 S.E.2d 675 (1950). The rigid requirement that the declarant must actually have died, State v. Dawson, 203 S.C. 167, 26 S.E.2d 506 (1943), is relaxed under the Rule which only requires the death of the declarant in a homicide prosecution. Subsection (3) is consistent with South Carolina law. State v. Doctor, 306 S.C. 527, 413 S.E.2d 36 (1992). Subsection (4) is consistent with South Carolina law. McLain v. Woodside, 95 S.C. 152, 79 S.E. 1 (1913).

Explanation

Even if it is hearsay, we will still let it in if it falls under one of these four exceptions. However, because these types of hearsay are not as reliable as the previous exceptions (803), then the rules require the party to show why the declarant is not available to explain why he said what he said. The three most common exceptions:

❖ Former testimony under oath in court

❖ Statement when he thought he was about to die

❖ Statement against interest

The reasoning: why would someone lie if they are under oath, thought they were going to die, or say something negative about themselves?

Also look to *Crawford* for Sixth Amendment issues (Rule 803 above).

Case Law

Former testimony

"Because Sanders had sufficient opportunity and motive to develop Vigier's testimony during the original trial to satisfy the requirements of Rule 804 (b)(1), SCRE and because Vigier was unavailable, the court properly admitted Vigier's prior testimony in the re-trial. As such, Sanders' right of confrontation was not violated."
State v. Sanders, 356 S.C. 214, 219, 588 S.E.2d 142, 145 (Ct. App. 2003)

Imminent Death

"Imminent is defined as '[n]ear at hand; mediate rather than immediate; close rather than touching; impending; on the point of happening; threatening; menacing; perilous.' '[D]ying declarations are competent evidence, for or against the accused, upon preliminary proof of certain conditions.' The rules in regard to such testimony are well settled: 1st. That death must be imminent at the time the declarations in question are made. 2nd. That the declarant must be so fully aware of this as to be without any hope of life. And 3rd. That the 'subject of the charge' must be the death of the declarant, and the circumstances of the death must be the subject of the declarations."
State v. Brown, 421 S.C. 337, 344 (Ct. App. 2017) (citations omitted)

Statement Against Interest

"Rule 804(b)(3), SCRE, requires the trial judge to view the disputed evidence in light of the surrounding circumstances and discern whether each particular remark is plainly self-

inculpatory. This entails a searching examination of both content and context."
State v. Young, 420 S.C. 608, 619 (Ct. App. 2017)

"The most faithful reading of Rule 804(b)(3)—which renders admissible 'statement[s] which ... so far ten[d] to subject the declarant to ... criminal liability ... that a reasonable person ... would not have made [them] unless believing [them] to be true'—is that it does not allow admission of non-self-inculpatory statements, even if they are made within a broader narrative that is generally self-inculpatory. Although the statutory term 'statement' can mean either an extended declaration or a single remark, the principle behind the Rule, so far as it is discernible from the text, points clearly to the narrower reading, so that only those remarks within a confession that are individually self-inculpatory are covered. The Rule is founded on the commonsense notion that reasonable people, even those who are not especially honest, tend not to make self-inculpatory statements unless they believe them to be true. This notion does not extend to a confession's non-self-inculpatory parts—to parts that are actually self-exculpatory, or to collateral statements, even ones that are neutral as to interest. A district court may not just assume that a statement is self-inculpatory because it is part of a fuller confession, especially when the statement implicates someone else."
Williamson v. United States, 512 U.S. 594 (1994)

RULE 805
HEARSAY WITHIN HEARSAY

Hearsay included within hearsay is not excluded under the hearsay rule if each part of the combined statements conforms with an exception to the hearsay rule provided in these rules.

Note:

The rule is identical to the federal rule and is consistent with prior South Carolina case law. Bain v. Self Memorial Hosp., 281 S.C. 138, 314 S.E.2d 603 (Ct. App. 1984).

Case Law

"The challenged testimony in this case—that the victim said Burroughs began the assault by asking for a hug—would more precisely be called double hearsay, or hearsay within hearsay. Under Rule 805, '[h]earsay included within hearsay is not excluded under the hearsay rule if each part of the combined statements conforms with an exception to the hearsay rule provided in these rules.' "
State v. Burroughs, 328 S.C. 489, 498, 492 S.E.2d 408, 412 (Ct. App. 1997)

"It might appear at first blush that the statement of Mrs. Murphy is a classic example of hearsay within hearsay or 'double hearsay' (*i.e.,* the statement of Mr. Murphy to Mrs. Murphy and the statement of Mrs. Murphy to Mrs. Beadle). *See Bain v. Self Memorial Hospital,* 281 S.C. 138, 145, 314 S.E.2d 603, 608 (Ct.App.1984) ('[H]earsay included within hearsay is not excluded from evidence if each part of the combined statements falls within some exception to the rule against hearsay.'). However, such is not the case because it does not appear that the statement of Mr. Murphy was offered in evidence to prove the truth of the matter asserted (*i.e.,* that he would in fact pay a fine for Mrs. Murphy and get her out of jail if she would assault Mrs. Yaeger)."

Yaeger v. Murphy, 291 S.C. 485, 491, 354 S.E.2d 393, 396 (Ct. App. 1987)

RULE 806
ATTACKING AND SUPPORTING CREDIBILITY OF
DECLARANT

When a hearsay statement, or a statement defined in Rule 801(d)(2)(C), (D), or (E) has been admitted in evidence, the credibility of the declarant may be attacked, and if attacked may be supported, by any evidence which would be admissible for those purposes if declarant had testified as a witness. Evidence of a statement or conduct by the declarant at any time, inconsistent with the declarant's hearsay statement, is not subject to any requirement that the declarant may have been afforded an opportunity to deny or explain. If the party against whom a hearsay statement has been admitted calls the declarant as a witness, the party is entitled to examine the declarant on the statement as if under cross-examination.

Note:

The rule is identical to the federal rule. However, it is a departure from prior South Carolina case law. There are cases which have addressed a similar matter by holding that a declarant who made a dying declaration could not be impeached with an inconsistent statement that did not independently fall within a hearsay exception. State v. Brown, 108 S.C. 490, 95 S.E. 61 (1918); State v. Taylor, 56 S.C. 360, 34 S.E. 939 (1900).

Explanation

A hearsay statement, by definition, means that the person who said the statement is not at trial to testify. However, even though they are not present, they can still be impeached just as if they were present and a witness. They can be impeached under 608, 609, and 613.

Keep in mind, the point of this rule is to allow a party to attack a witness's credibility, not to get substantive evidence in.

Also keep in mind, if a party calls a witness and that witness testifies to a statement made by the party opponent, then can the same party who called that witness go ahead and impeach the party opponent? The case law isn't clear, but it is an issue to look out for. If a party calls a witness and that witness gives a hearsay statement from that same party (would need to be hearsay exception, because it wouldn't be party opponent statement), then the opposing party would be able to impeach the opposing party at this point, even though they have not actually taken the witness stand.

Case Law

"The basis for this rule is obvious. As the Federal Rules of Evidence Advisory Committee said: 'The declarant of a hearsay statement which is admitted in evidence is in effect a witness. His credibility should in fairness be subject to impeachment and support as though he had in fact testified. See Rules 608 and 609.' By introducing the hearsay statements made by Moss, the prosecution put Moss' credibility in issue. Prior inconsistent statements are a well recognized means of impeaching a witness. FRE Rule 613.[1] The secretary's testimony, which would have included conversations showing Moss had stated that Brainard and Bittick did not know the true nature of TVM, would have been such an inconsistent statement. As such, it would have been admissible under Rule 806, and failure to admit it was reversible error."
United States v. Brainard, 690 F.2d 1117, 1128 (4th Cir. 1982)

157

"But while Fed.R.Evid. 806 provides that the credibility of the declarant of a hearsay statement may be attacked by any evidence which would be admissible for that purpose if the declarant had testified as a witness, *e.g.* by evidence of bias, interest, prejudice, prior conviction of a crime, or inconsistent statements, the rule does not apply to statements which are not hearsay."
United States v. Sadler, 48 F.3d 1218 (4th Cir. 1995)

"Rule 806 applies to hearsay statements and certain statements offered against an opposing party that have 'been admitted in evidence.' Fed.R.Evid. 806. By its terms, Rule 806 was not the mechanism for admission of Tsoa's written out-of-court statements contained in the emails. Further, Tsoa's counsel offered the emails as probative of Tsoa's knowledge and abilities, not as bearing on credibility."
United States v. Ging-Hwang Tsoa, 592 F. App'x 153, 157 (4th Cir. 2014)

"Although the rule does not expressly include attempts to attack a defendant's out-of-court statements admitted pursuant to Fed.R.Evid. 801(d)(2)(A), the Senate Judiciary Committee's report concerning the proposed rules states:

> The committee considered it unnecessary to include statements contained in Rule 801(d)(2)(A) and (B)-the statement by the party-opponent himself or the statement of which he has manifested his adoption- because the credibility of the party-opponent is always subject to an attack on his credibility."

United States v. Shay, 57 F.3d 126, 132 (1st Cir. 1995)

Impeaching defendant

"The defendant Charles William Lawson appeals from his jury conviction for uttering and possessing counterfeit money. He contends that the district court committed reversible error in permitting the jury to hear evidence of two previous convictions. Though Lawson did not testify, his counsel cross-examined a government witness who was a secret service agent to bring out the fact that Lawson had consistently denied any involvement, and introduced a written statement in which Lawson denied all complicity in the counterfeit activities.

By putting these hearsay statements before the jury his counsel made Lawson's credibility an issue in the case the same as if Lawson had made the statements from the witness stand…

Thus, evidence which would have been admissible to impeach Lawson if he had testified was admissible for this purpose under the circumstances of this case. Prior felony convictions are admissible for this purpose under Rule 609(a), Fed.R.Evid. The jury was properly instructed that the evidence of previous convictions was to be considered only on the issue of credibility."

United States v. Lawson, 608 F.2d 1129, 1129–30 (6th Cir. 1979)

Article IX. Authentication and Identification

RULE 901
REQUIREMENT OF AUTHENTICATION OR IDENTIFICATION

(a) General Provision. The requirement of authentication or identification as a condition precedent to admissibility is satisfied by evidence sufficient to support a finding that the matter in question is what its proponent claims.

(b) Illustrations. By way of illustration only, and not by way of limitation, the following are examples of authentication or identification conforming with the requirements of this rule:

> **(1) Testimony of Witness With Knowledge.** Testimony that a matter is what it is claimed to be.

> **(2) Nonexpert Opinion on Handwriting.** Non-expert opinion as to the genuineness of handwriting, based upon familiarity not acquired for purposes of the litigation.

> **(3) Comparison by Trier or Expert Witness.** Comparison by the trier of fact or by expert witnesses with specimens which have been authenticated.

> **(4) Distinctive Characteristics and the Like.** Appearance, contents, substance, internal patterns, or other distinctive characteristics, taken in conjunction with circumstances.

(5) Voice Identification. Identification of a voice, whether heard firsthand or through mechanical or electronic transmission or recording, by opinion based upon hearing the voice at any time under circumstances connecting it with the alleged speaker.

(6)   Telephone   Conversations. Telephone conversations, by evidence that a call was made to the number assigned at the time by the telephone company to a particular person or business, if (A) in the case of a person, circumstances, including self-identification, show the person answering to be the one called, or (B) in the case of a business, the call was made to a place of business and the conversation related to business reasonably transacted over the telephone.

(7) Public Records or Reports. Evidence that a writing authorized by law to be recorded or filed and in fact recorded or filed in a public office, or a purported public record, report, statement, or data compilation, in any form, is from the public office where items of this nature are kept.

(8)   Ancient   Documents   or   Data Compilation. Evidence that a document or data compilation, in any form, (A) is in such condition as to create no suspicion concerning its authenticity, (B) was in a place where it, if authentic, would likely be, and (C) has been in existence 20 years or more at the time it is offered.

(9) Process or System. Evidence describing a process or system used to produce a result and showing that the process or system produces an accurate result.

(10) Methods Provided by Statute or Rule. Any method of authentication or identification provided by statute or by other rules promulgated by the Supreme Court.

Note:

In considering the rules in Article IX, it is important to remember that these rules relate to how a party authenticates evidence to show it is what the party claims. Even when evidence is properly authenticated, it must still be admissible under the other rules of evidence. See State v. Jeffcoat, 279 S.C. 167, 303 S.E.2d 855 (1983).

With the exception of subsection (b)(10) which is discussed below, this rule is identical to the federal rule.

Subsection (a) is consistent with South Carolina law which requires authentication as a condition precedent to admissibility. See State v. Rich, 293 S.C. 172, 359 S.E.2d 281 (1987). As noted in the Advisory Committee's Notes to the Federal Rules, the requirement of showing authentication or identity falls in the category of relevancy dependent upon fulfillment of a condition of fact and is governed by the procedure set forth in Rule 104(b).

Subsection (b) contains illustrations of how evidence may be authenticated. These illustrations are consistent with the prior case law indicating that evidence in support of authentication can be direct or circumstantial. Winburn v. Minnesota Mutual Life Ins. Co., 261 S.C. 568, 201 S.E.2d 372 (1973); State v. Wilson, 246 S.C. 580, 145 S.E.2d 20 (1965).

162

Subsection (b)(1) is in accord with the prior law in this state. Williams v. Milling-Nelson Motors, Inc., 209 S.C. 407, 40 S.E.2d 633 (1946); Brazeale v. Piedmont Mfg. Co., 184 S.C. 471, 193 S.E. 99 (1937).

Subsection (b)(2) is generally consistent with state law State v. Jeffcoat, 279 S.C. 167, 303 S.E.2d 855 (1983) (signature on check identified by signator's bookkeeper); Weaver v. Whilden, 33 S.C. 190, 11 S.E. 686 (1890) (no error in refusing to allow nonexpert witness who was unfamiliar with handwriting to testify as to genuineness of signature). There does not appear to be any South Carolina law that states that the familiarity cannot have been acquired for the purposes of litigation.

Subsection (b)(3) is in accord with the prior case law in South Carolina. Pee Dee Production Credit Ass'n v. Joye, 284 S.C. 371, 326 S.E.2d 650 (1984); Benedict, Hall & Co. v. Flanigan, 18 S.C. 506 (1883); Boman v. Plunkett, 13 S.C.L. (2 McCord) 518 (1823) (comparison by jury was permitted in aid of doubtful proof). South Carolina has also recognized that nonexperts can make such comparisons. State v. Ezekial, 33 S.C. 115, 11 S.E. 635 (1890); Benedict, Hall & Co. v. Flanigan, 18 S.C. 506 (1883).

Subsection (b)(4) is consistent with prior law. Kershaw, Cty. Bd. of Educ. v. U.S. Gypsum, 302 S.C. 390, 396 S.E.2d 369 (1990); IKT Company Inc. v. Hardwick, 274 S.C. 413, 265 S.E.2d 510 (1980); State v. Hightower, 221 S.C. 91, 69 S.E.2d 363 (1952). A common form of authentication permissible under this subsection is the reply doctrine which provides that once a letter, telegram, or telephone call is shown to have been mailed, sent, or made, a letter, telegram or telephone call shown by its contents to be in reply is authenticated without more. Graham, Handbook of Federal Evidence, §

163

901.4 (2nd ed. 1986). This appears to be the law in South Carolina.Leesville Mfg. Co. v. Morgan Wood & Iron Works, 75 S.C. 342, 55 S.E. 768 (1906) (reply letter is presumed genuine).

Subsection (b)(5) is consistent with the law in South Carolina. State v. Stewart, 275 S.C. 447, 272 S.E.2d 628 (1980) (identification of defendant's voice as that of armed robber was admissible in criminal prosecution where circumstances demonstrate reliability of evidence); State v. Plyler, 275 S.C. 291, 270 S.E.2d 126 (1980) (sufficient testimony as to recognition of the voice warrants its admission); State v. Vice, 259 S.C. 30, 190 S.E.2d 510 (1972) (voice identification permissible; further, jury can compare recorded telephone call and defendant's voice, recorded prior to trial, for purposes of comparison); State v. Porter, 251 S.C. 393, 162 S.E.2d 843 (1968) (identification of party with whom witness talked need not be known at time of conversation, but is sufficient if knowledge enabling witness to identify other party is later obtained), cert. denied, 393 U.S. 1079, 89 S.Ct. 859, 21 L.Ed.2d 773 (1969); State v. Steadman, 216 S.C. 579, 59 S.E.2d 168 (1950); State v. Smith, 307 S.C. 376, 415 S.E.2d 409 (Ct.App.1992) (dispatcher allowed to identify voice of anonymous caller as that of defendant, even though no prior voice identification training).

Subsection (b)(6) is in accord with the prior law in this State. Fielding Home for Funerals v. Pub. Sav. Life Ins. Co., 271 S.C. 117, 245 S.E.2d 238 (1978) (business); State v. Steadman, 216 S.C. 579, 59 S.E.2d 168 (1950); Gilliland & Gaffney v. Southern Ry., 85 S.C. 26, 67 S.E. 20 (1910) (business).

Section (b)(7) is consistent with South Carolina law. State v. Pearson, 223 S.C. 377, 76 S.E.2d 151 (1953); Ex parte Steen,

164

59 S.C. 220, 37 S.E. 829 (1901). As to the authentication of police fingerprint records, see State v. Rich, 293 S.C. 172, 359 S.E.2d 281 (1987).

Subsection (b)(8) is in accord with prior case law with the exception that the prior cases required 30 years before a document was classified as ancient rather than 20 years as required by this subsection. See Atlantic Coast Line Ry. v. Searson, 137 S.C. 468, 135 S.E. 567 (1926); Polson v. Ingram, 22 S.C. 541 (1885); Thompson v. Brannon, 14 S.C. 542 (1881); Johnson v. Pritchard, 302 S.C. 437, 395 S.E.2d 191 (Ct. App. 1990). See also, Rule 803(16), which also reduces the minimum period for receipt of "ancient" records under the hearsay rule.

Subsection (b)(9) appears to be in accord with South Carolina law. See State v. Hester, 137 S.C. 145, 134 S.E.2d 885 (1926).

Subsection (b)(10) is the federal rule modified to make the language applicable to South Carolina statutes and rules. An example of such a rule is Rule 44, SCRCP, which deals with the authentication of official records.

Explanation

Authentication is the method used to make sure a piece of evidence is what it is claimed to be. It is merely the first condition that must be met before allowing a piece of evidence in. This rule lays out some examples of how a piece of evidence can be verified. This list is not exhaustive. These are just some examples.

Case Law

"As discussed by the Court of Appeals, *Rich* does not establish an authentication requirement that necessitates the testimony of the actual person who took the fingerprints on the master fingerprint card. Instead, it merely requires 'evidence as to *when and by whom* the card was made and that the prints on the card were in fact those of this defendant.

Although not exhaustive, Rule 901 further provides examples of authentication or identification which conform with the requirements of the rule. We find several of these illustrations are applicable in the instant case."

State v. Anderson, 386 S.C. 120, 128 (2009) (citations omitted)

Distinctive Characteristics

"First, subsection four provides that a proponent of physical evidence may satisfy the threshold authentication requirement of Rule 901(a) by 'internal patterns, or other distinctive characteristics, taken in conjunction with circumstances.' Here, Sergeant Gause, an expert in the field of fingerprint analysis, analyzed the latent fingerprints found at the Wards' home by checking them through the AFIS. Using this technology and comparing the characteristics of the latent fingerprints with those of the known prints, Gause determined that Anderson's known prints matched the latent prints. Gause further explained that the prints on the master fingerprint card were taken at a correctional facility, on a specific date, and assigned a unique state identifying number."

State v. Anderson, 386 S.C. 120, 129, 687 S.E.2d 35, 40 (2009)

Recorded in Public Office

"Second, subsection seven, the public records example.... Here, Lieutenant Means and Sergeant Gause testified that law enforcement takes the fingerprints of every person who is arrested in this state. SLED then receives and maintains these known prints on the ten-print card in the condition in which it arrives. The AFIS stores all of the digital fingerprint images of every ten-print card in South Carolina. We conclude this testimony established the fingerprint card of Anderson constituted a public report or record given its production was authorized by law to be recorded or filed at SLED."
State v. Anderson, 386 S.C. 120, 129, 687 S.E.2d 35, 40 (2009)

Process or System

"Third ... authentication by '[e]vidence describing a process or system used to produce a result and showing that the process or system produces an accurate result.' The State in this case presented evidence regarding: when and where Anderson's fingerprints were taken; how they were submitted to SLED; the process implemented by law enforcement for taking the fingerprints; and how an accurate record of them was maintained in the AFIS. We hold this testimony satisfied the authentication requirement of Rule 901."
State v. Anderson, 386 S.C. 120, 129, 687 S.E.2d 35, 40 (2009)

Generalized Approach

"Even if the evidence presented by the State did not precisely fit within one of the enumerated examples provided in Rule 901, we find Anderson's known ten-print card was, nevertheless, authenticated under a more generalized approach to Rule 901. The State provided expert testimony which linked the latent fingerprints with Anderson's known prints. Sergeant Gause, who was qualified as an expert in the field of fingerprint analysis, testified regarding the method and technology in which he analyzed the latent fingerprints with the known prints. This testimony included a thorough explanation of how an arrestee's fingerprints are taken, stored, and maintained. Using the officially-maintained known fingerprints, Gause opined that the latent print found at the Wards' home matched Anderson's known print in the AFIS database. Thus, this expert testimony was sufficient 'to support a finding that the matter in question [was] what [the State] claim[ed].' "

State v. Anderson, 386 S.C. 120, 129, 687 S.E.2d 35, 40 (2009)

RULE 902
SELF-AUTHENTICATION

Extrinsic evidence of authenticity as a condition precedent to admissibility is not required with respect to the following:

(1) Domestic Public Documents Under Seal. A document bearing a seal purporting to be that of the United States, or of any State, district, Commonwealth, territory, or insular possession thereof, or the Panama Canal Zone, or the Trust Territory of the Pacific Islands, or of a political subdivision, department, officer, or agency thereof, and a signature purporting to be an attestation or execution.

(2) Domestic Public Documents Not Under Seal. A document purporting to bear the signature in the official capacity of an officer or employee of any entity included in subsection (1) hereof, having no seal, if a public officer having a seal and having official duties in the district or political subdivision of the officer or employee certifies under seal that the signer has the official capacity and that the signature is genuine.

(3) Foreign Public Documents. A document purporting to be executed or attested in an official capacity by a person authorized by the laws of a foreign country to make the execution or attestation, and accompanied by a final certification as to the genuineness of the signature and official position (A) of the executing or attesting person, or (B) of any foreign official whose certificate of genuineness of signature and official position relates to the execution or attestation or is in a chain of certificates of genuineness of signature and official position relating to the execution or attestation. A final certification may be made by a secretary of embassy or legation, consul general, consul, vice consul, or consular agent of the United States, or a diplomatic or consular official of the foreign country assigned or accredited to the United States. If reasonable opportunity has been given to all parties to investigate the authenticity and accuracy of official documents, the court may, for good cause shown, order that they be treated as presumptively authentic without final certification or permit them to be evidenced by an attested summary with or without final certification.

(4) Certified Copies of Public Records. A copy of an official record or report or entry therein, or of a document authorized by law to be recorded or filed and actually recorded or filed in a public office, including data compilations in any form, certified as correct by the custodian or other person authorized to make the certification, by certificate complying with subsection (1), (2), or (3) of this rule or complying with any statute or rule promulgated by the Supreme Court.

(5) Official Publications. Books, pamphlets, or other publications purporting to be issued by public authority.

(6) Newspapers and Periodicals. Printed materials purporting to be newspapers or periodicals.

(7) Trade Inscriptions and the Like. Inscriptions, signs, tags, or labels purporting to have been affixed in the course of business and indicating ownership, control, or origin.

(8) Acknowledged Documents. Documents accompanied by a certificate of acknowledgment executed in the manner provided by law by a notary public or other officer authorized by law to take acknowledgments.

(9) Commercial Paper and Related Documents. Commercial paper, signatures thereon, and documents relating thereto to the extent provided by general commercial law.

(10) Presumptions Under Statutes. Any signature, document or other matter declared by statute to be presumptively or prima facie genuine or authentic.

Note:

With the exception of subsections (4) and (10) which are discussed below, this rule is identical to the federal rule.

Subsection (1): South Carolina law has previously permitted self-authentication of certain classes of domestic public documents under seal. See e.g., S.C. Code Ann. § 19-5-220 (1985) (proof of various documents under seal of any city or state).

Subsection (2): There does not appear to be any South Carolina law permitting self-authentication in these circumstances.

Subsection (3) is similar to Rule 44(a)(2), SCRCP.

Subsection (4) is identical to the federal rule except that it is amended so as to also allow compliance with "any statute or rule prescribed by the Supreme Court." Examples of such statutes and rules include: S.C. Code Ann. § 19-5-10 (1985) (admissibility of certified copies or certified photostatic copies of documents); S.C. Code Ann. § 19-5-30 (Supp. 1993) (admissibility of photostatic or certified copies of certain motor vehicle records); Rule 44(a)(1), SCRCP (authentication of domestic records); Rule 6, SCRCrimP (self-authentication of chemist's or analyst's report of nature of "controlled dangerous substances").

Subsection (5): There does not appear to be any South Carolina authority for this proposition.

Subsection (6) appears to be consistent with South Carolina law. See Kirkpatrick v. Hardeman, 123 S.C. 21, 115 S.E. 905 (1923) (although unclear if Court treated as hearsay or authentication problem, newspaper reports of stock quotations were admitted for purpose of proving market value of stock).

Subsection (7): There does not appear to be any South Carolina authority for this proposition.

Subsection (8): This is similar to South Carolina Code Ann. §§ 19-5-220 and 19-5-230 (1985) which allow the self-authentication of certain documents of city, state or foreign governments under seal of a notary public.

Subsection (9): Under the Uniform Commercial Code, certain items are self-authenticating. See S.C. Code Ann. § 36-1-202 (1976) (includes bills of lading, insurance policies or any document authorized by the contract to be issued by third party); § 36-3-307 (1976) (signatures, unless specifically denied in the pleadings); § 36-3-510 (1976) (formal certificate of protest, a stamp by drawee that payment was refused, or bank records showing dishonor are all admissible in evidence and create a presumption of dishonor); § 36-8-105(3) (Supp. 1993) (signatures on a certificated security, in a necessary indorsement, on an initial transaction statement or on an instruction is admitted unless put into issue).

Subsection (10): This subsection differs from the federal rule only in that "declared by statute" is substituted for "declared by Act of Congress." An example of a statute under this subsection is S.C. Code Ann. § 39-15-140 (1985) (certificate of trademark registration issued by the Secretary of State).

Explanation

Some pieces of evidence do not need anything to prove that it is what it claims to be. So if the piece of evidence falls under one of the 10 categories in this rule, then that piece of evidence is automatically authenticated. That does not mean it automatically comes into evidence. Merely, it passes the first test.

Case Law

"'[T]he burden to authenticate ... is not high' and requires only that the proponent 'offer[ ] a satisfactory foundation from which the jury could reasonably find that the evidence is authentic.' 29A Am. Jur. 2d *Evidence* § 1045 (2008) ('The authentication requirement does not demand that the proponent of ... evidence conclusively demonstrate [its] genuineness....')."
Deep Keel, LLC v. Atl. Private Equity Grp., LLC, 413 S.C. 58, 64–65 (Ct. App. 2015) (citation omitted)

"[W]e find the first five loan documents—excluding the partial release—are self-authenticating under Rule 902(9), which provides, 'Extrinsic evidence of authenticity as a condition precedent to admissibility is not required with respect to ... [c]ommercial paper, signatures thereon, and documents relating thereto to the extent provided by general commercial law.' The note is commercial paper, and the other four loan documents are either commercial paper themselves

or 'documents relating thereto.' Each of the five documents bears the signature of Terry L. Rohlfing."
Deep Keel, LLC v. Atl. Private Equity Grp., LLC, 413 S.C. 58, 67 (Ct. App. 2015) (citation omitted)

RULE 903
SUBSCRIBING WITNESS' TESTIMONY UNNECESSARY

The testimony of a subscribing witness is not necessary to authenticate a writing unless required by statute or by the laws of the jurisdiction whose laws govern the validity of the writing.

Note:

This rule adds "by statute" to the federal rule. The law in South Carolina is that the testimony of a subscribing witness is generally not necessary for authentication. Edgar v. Brown, 15 S.C.L. (4 McCord) 91 (1827); S.C. Code Ann. § 19-1-120 (1985) (the absence of a witness to any bond or note shall not be deemed a good cause by any court for postponing a trial, but the signature may be proved by other testimony); S.C. Code Ann. § 62-2-503 (Supp. 1993) (Uniform Probate Code's provision for self-proved wills); §§ 62-3-405 and -406 (Supp. 1993) (requirements of proof of execution when will not self-proved and submitted for formal probate).

Article X. Contents of Writings, Recordings, and Photographs

RULE 1001
DEFINITIONS

For purposes of this article the following definitions are applicable:

(1) Writings and Recordings. "Writings" and "recordings" consist of letters, words, sounds, or numbers, or their equivalent, set down by handwriting, typewriting, printing, photostating, photographing, magnetic impulse, mechanical or electronic recording, or other form of data compilation.

(2) Photographs. "Photographs" include still photographs, X-ray films, video tapes, motion pictures or other similar methods of recording information.

(3) Original. An "original" of a writing or recording is the writing or recording itself or any counterpart intended to have the same effect by a person executing or issuing it. An "original" of a photograph includes the negative or any print therefrom. If data are stored in a computer or similar device, any printout or other output readable by sight, shown to reflect the data accurately, is an "original".

(4) Duplicate. A "duplicate" is a counterpart produced by the same impression as the original, or from the same matrix, or by means of photography, including enlargements and miniatures, or by mechanical or electronic re-recording, or by chemical reproduction, or by other equivalent techniques which accurately reproduces the original.

Note:

This rule is identical to the federal rule except that the word "sounds" is added to subdivision (1) and "other similar methods of recording information" was added to subdivision (2). This additional language does not significantly alter the rule, and provides for advances in technology.

Case Law

"We find the photographs from the disk were originals pursuant to Rule 1001 ('If data are stored in a computer or similar device, any printout or other output readable by sight, shown to reflect the data accurately, is an original.'). A digital camera was used, and the photographs from the disk were testified to as being the same photographs that were on the deer camera on October 28, 2008. Mitchell had the opportunity to cross-examine Potts and the police officers as to the handling of the photographs and disk on which the photographs were downloaded. We conclude the trial court properly admitted the photographs from the disk as originals, and thus, Rule 1003 is not relevant to our analysis."
State v. Mitchell, 399 S.C. 410, 421–22 (Ct. App. 2012) (citations omitted)

"Because there is simply no way of knowing, by merely reading this contract, what Cleckley was supposed to do after it finished re-paving the road, we find the testimony was properly admitted to explain it.[4]
4
We reject Department's argument that the best evidence rule was violated in this case. This rule provides that when the contents of a writing are sought to be proved, the original document must be produced unless some reason can be shown

for its unavailability. The best evidence rule has no application here because the contract was introduced into evidence. Furthermore, this objectionable testimony was not introduced to state what the contract terms were but to show how the parties interpreted them."

Penton v. J.F. Cleckley & Co., 326 S.C. 275, 281–82 (1997) (citation omitted)

"Here, the trial court excluded evidence of the letter finding that it was unreliable and inadmissible under the best evidence rule—Rules 1001 to 1004, SCRE.[4] Rule 1002, SCRE, provides: 'To prove the content of a writing, recording, or photograph, the original writing, recording, or photograph is required, except as otherwise provided in these rules or by statute.' Further, Rule 1004, SCRE, states in relevant part: 'The original is not required, and other evidence of the contents of a writing, recording, or photograph is admissible if—[ ] All originals are lost or have been destroyed, unless the proponent lost or destroyed them in bad faith.'

The trial court erred in excluding evidence of Cottrell's letter to Counts under the best evidence rule.[5] The record does not reveal that the original letter was destroyed through any bad faith of the proponent; thus, there was no basis for excluding Counts' statements about the letter under the best evidence rule."

State v. Halcomb, 382 S.C. 432, 443–44, 676 S.E.2d 149, 155 (Ct. App. 2009)

RULE 1002
REQUIREMENT OF ORIGINAL

To prove the content of a writing, recording, or photograph, the original writing, recording, or photograph is required, except as otherwise provided in these rules or by statute.

Note:

This rule is better known as the best evidence rule. This rule is identical to the federal rule except the words "by statute" were substituted at the end of the rule in place of the words "by Act of Congress."

The proposed rule is consistent with current case law as it applies to writings. See, e.g., Riddle v. City of Greenville, 251 S.C. 473, 163 S.E.2d 462 (1968); Sample v. Gulf Refining Co., 183 S.C. 399, 191 S.E. 209 (1937); Cain v. Whitlock, 178 S.C. 289, 182 S.E. 752 (1935); Mull v. Easley Lumber Co., 121 S.C. 155, 113 S.E. 356 (1922); Guinarin v. So. Life & Trust Co., 106 S.C. 37, 90 S.E. 319 (1916); Mayfield v. So. Ry., 85 S.C. 165, 67 S.E. 132 (1910); McCoy v. Atl. Coast Line Ry., 84 S.C. 62, 65 S.E. 939 (1909).

There are no cases which deal with the applicability of the best evidence rule to photographs and only one case in which the best evidence rule has been applied to recordings. State v. Worthy, 239 S.C. 449, 123 S.E.2d 835 (1962), overruled on other grounds, State v. Torrence, 305 S.C. 45, 406 S.E.2d 315 (1991).

Examples of statutes that have an effect on the requirement to produce the original are: S.C. Code Ann. § 19-1-110 (1985) (instruments of common carriers); S.C. Code Ann. § 19-5-10

(1985) (public documents); S.C. Code Ann. § 19-5-210 (1985) (grants issued by North Carolina); S.C. Code Ann. §§ 19-5-310 and -320 (1985) (missing person reports); S.C. Code Ann. § 19-5-510 (1985) (business records).

Explanation

Remember, the best evidence rule only applies to writings, recordings or photographs. And it also only applies if the witness is trying to prove the actual content of one of those.

The first question with an objection to not having best evidence, is the document the original? If it is not the original, then it is it a photocopy or duplicate? The duplicate will generally come in, unless there is an issue to its authenticity.

If it is not the original and it is not a duplicate, then does an exception apply?

Case Law

"We find the photographs from the disk were originals pursuant to Rule 1001 ('If data are stored in a computer or similar device, any printout or other output readable by sight, shown to reflect the data accurately, is an original.'). A digital camera was used, and the photographs from the disk were testified to as being the same photographs that were on the deer camera on October 28, 2008. Mitchell had the opportunity to cross-examine Potts and the police officers as to the handling of the photographs and disk on which the photographs were downloaded. We conclude the trial court properly admitted the photographs from the disk as originals, and thus, Rule 1003 is not relevant to our analysis."
State v. Mitchell, 399 S.C. 410, 421–22 (Ct. App. 2012) (citations omitted)

"Because there is simply no way of knowing, by merely reading this contract, what Cleckley was supposed to do after it finished re-paving the road, we find the testimony was properly admitted to explain it.[4]

4

We reject Department's argument that the best evidence rule was violated in this case. This rule provides that when the contents of a writing are sought to be proved, the original document must be produced unless some reason can be shown for its unavailability. The best evidence rule has no application here because the contract was introduced into evidence. Furthermore, this objectionable testimony was not introduced to state what the contract terms were but to show how the parties interpreted them."

Penton v. J.F. Cleckley & Co., 326 S.C. 275, 281–82 (1997) (citation omitted)

"Here, the trial court excluded evidence of the letter finding that it was unreliable and inadmissible under the best evidence rule—Rules 1001 to 1004, SCRE.[4] Rule 1002, SCRE, provides: 'To prove the content of a writing, recording, or photograph, the original writing, recording, or photograph is required, except as otherwise provided in these rules or by statute.' Further, Rule 1004, SCRE, states in relevant part: 'The original is not required, and other evidence of the contents of a writing, recording, or photograph is admissible if—[ ] All originals are lost or have been destroyed, unless the proponent lost or destroyed them in bad faith.'

The trial court erred in excluding evidence of Cottrell's letter to Counts under the best evidence rule.[5] The record does not reveal that the original letter was destroyed through any bad faith of the proponent; thus, there was no basis for excluding Counts' statements about the letter under the best evidence rule."

State v. Halcomb, 382 S.C. 432, 443–44, 676 S.E.2d 149, 155 (Ct. App. 2009)

RULE 1003
ADMISSIBILITY OF DUPLICATES

A duplicate is admissible to the same extent as an original unless (1) a genuine question is raised as to the authenticity of the original or (2) in the circumstances it would be unfair to admit the duplicate in lieu of the original.

Note:

This rule is identical to the federal rule. There is no case law in this State on the admissibility of a duplicate in this context, only on the admissibility of a duplicate as secondary evidence. See Note following Rule 1004.

Case Law

"We find the photographs from the disk were originals pursuant to Rule 1001 ('If data are stored in a computer or similar device, any printout or other output readable by sight, shown to reflect the data accurately, is an original.'). A digital camera was used, and the photographs from the disk were testified to as being the same photographs that were on the deer camera on October 28, 2008. Mitchell had the opportunity to cross-examine Potts and the police officers as to the handling of the photographs and disk on which the photographs were downloaded. We conclude the trial court properly admitted the photographs from the disk as originals, and thus, Rule 1003 is not relevant to our analysis."
State v. Mitchell, 399 S.C. 410, 421–22 (Ct. App. 2012) (citations omitted)

"Because there is simply no way of knowing, by merely reading this contract, what Cleckley was supposed to do after it finished re-paving the road, we find the testimony was properly admitted to explain it.[4]

4

We reject Department's argument that the best evidence rule was violated in this case. This rule provides that when the contents of a writing are sought to be proved, the original document must be produced unless some reason can be shown for its unavailability. The best evidence rule has no application here because the contract was introduced into evidence. Furthermore, this objectionable testimony was not introduced to state what the contract terms were but to show how the parties interpreted them."

Penton v. J.F. Cleckley & Co., 326 S.C. 275, 281–82 (1997) (citation omitted)

"Here, the trial court excluded evidence of the letter finding that it was unreliable and inadmissible under the best evidence rule—Rules 1001 to 1004, SCRE.[4] Rule 1002, SCRE, provides: 'To prove the content of a writing, recording, or photograph, the original writing, recording, or photograph is required, except as otherwise provided in these rules or by statute.' Further, Rule 1004, SCRE, states in relevant part: 'The original is not required, and other evidence of the contents of a writing, recording, or photograph is admissible if—[ ] All originals are lost or have been destroyed, unless the proponent lost or destroyed them in bad faith.'

The trial court erred in excluding evidence of Cottrell's letter to Counts under the best evidence rule.[5] The record does not reveal that the original letter was destroyed through any bad faith of the proponent; thus, there was no basis for excluding Counts' statements about the letter under the best evidence rule."

State v. Halcomb, 382 S.C. 432, 443–44, 676 S.E.2d 149, 155 (Ct. App. 2009)

RULE 1004

ADMISSIBILITY OF OTHER EVIDENCE OF CONTENTS

The original is not required, and other evidence of the contents of a writing, recording, or photograph is admissible if -

(1) Originals Lost or Destroyed. All originals are lost or have been destroyed, unless the proponent lost or destroyed them in bad faith; or

(2) Original Not Obtainable. No original can be obtained by any available judicial process or procedure; or

(3) Original in Possession of Opponent. At a time when an original was under the control of the party against whom offered, that party was put on notice, by the pleadings or otherwise, that the contents would be a subject of proof at the hearing, and that party does not produce the original at the hearing; or

(4) Collateral Matters. The writing, recording, or photograph is not closely related to a controlling issue.

Note:

This rule is identical to the federal rule and is consistent with our case law. It has long been the law in South Carolina that secondary evidence is admissible under the circumstances outlined in this rule. See, e.g., Pee Dee Prod. Credit Ass'n v. Love, 284 S.C. 371, 326 S.E.2d 650 (1984) (original lost); Windham v. Lloyd, 253 S.C. 568, 172 S.E.2d 117 (1970) (original lost); Wynn v. Coney, 232 S.C. 346, 102 S.E.2d 209 (1958) (original in possession of opponent); Greer v.

Equitable Life Assur. Soc'y, 180 S.C. 162, 185 S.E. 68 (1936) (collateral matter); Rose v. Winnsboro Nat'l Bank, 41 S.C. 191, 19 S.E. 487 (1894) (original in possession of opponent).

Case Law

"We find the photographs from the disk were originals pursuant to Rule 1001 ('If data are stored in a computer or similar device, any printout or other output readable by sight, shown to reflect the data accurately, is an original.'). A digital camera was used, and the photographs from the disk were testified to as being the same photographs that were on the deer camera on October 28, 2008. Mitchell had the opportunity to cross-examine Potts and the police officers as to the handling of the photographs and disk on which the photographs were downloaded. We conclude the trial court properly admitted the photographs from the disk as originals, and thus, Rule 1003 is not relevant to our analysis."
State v. Mitchell, 399 S.C. 410, 421–22 (Ct. App. 2012) (citations omitted)

"Because there is simply no way of knowing, by merely reading this contract, what Cleckley was supposed to do after it finished re-paving the road, we find the testimony was properly admitted to explain it.[4]
4
We reject Department's argument that the best evidence rule was violated in this case. This rule provides that when the contents of a writing are sought to be proved, the original document must be produced unless some reason can be shown for its unavailability. The best evidence rule has no application here because the contract was introduced into evidence. Furthermore, this objectionable testimony was not

187

introduced to state what the contract terms were but to show how the parties interpreted them."
Penton v. J.F. Cleckley & Co., 326 S.C. 275, 281–82 (1997) (citation omitted)

"Here, the trial court excluded evidence of the letter finding that it was unreliable and inadmissible under the best evidence rule—Rules 1001 to 1004, SCRE.[4] Rule 1002, SCRE, provides: 'To prove the content of a writing, recording, or photograph, the original writing, recording, or photograph is required, except as otherwise provided in these rules or by statute.' Further, Rule 1004, SCRE, states in relevant part: 'The original is not required, and other evidence of the contents of a writing, recording, or photograph is admissible if—[ ] All originals are lost or have been destroyed, unless the proponent lost or destroyed them in bad faith.'
The trial court erred in excluding evidence of Cottrell's letter to Counts under the best evidence rule.[5] The record does not reveal that the original letter was destroyed through any bad faith of the proponent; thus, there was no basis for excluding Counts' statements about the letter under the best evidence rule."
State v. Halcomb, 382 S.C. 432, 443–44, 676 S.E.2d 149, 155 (Ct. App. 2009)

RULE 1005
PUBLIC RECORDS

The contents of an official record, or of a document authorized to be recorded or filed and actually recorded or filed, including data compilations in any form, if otherwise admissible, may be proved by copy, certified as correct in accordance with Rule 902 or testified to be correct by a witness who has compared it with the original. If a copy which complies with the foregoing cannot be obtained by the exercise of reasonable diligence, then other evidence of the contents may be given.

Note:

This rule is identical to the federal rule and is substantially similar to S.C. Code Ann. § 19-5-10 (1985) and Rule 44, SCRCP.

Case Law

"A public record or report under this provision only requires that the document be produced and maintained in a public office. The fact that the general public does not have access to the document, i.e., fingerprint cards, does not negate this method of authentication. See S.C.Code Ann. § 30–4–20(c) (2007) (defining the term 'public record' to include 'documentary materials regardless of physical form or characteristics prepared ... or retained by a public body'); *see also* Rule 1005, SCRE ('The contents of an official record, or of a document authorized to be recorded or filed and actually recorded or filed, including data compilations in any form, if otherwise admissible, may be proved by copy, certified as correct in accordance with Rule 902 or testified to be correct by a witness who has compared it with the original. If a copy which complies with the foregoing cannot be obtained by the exercise of reasonable diligence, then other evidence of the contents may be given.').”

State v. Anderson, 386 S.C. 120, 131, 687 S.E.2d 35, 40 (2009)

SUMMARIES

The contents of voluminous writings, recordings, or photographs which cannot conveniently be examined in court may be presented in the form of a chart, summary, or calculation, provided the underlying data are admissible into evidence. The originals, or duplicates, shall be made available for examination or copying, or both, by other parties at reasonable time and place. The court may order that they be produced in court.

Note:

This rule is identical to the federal rule except for the language "provided the underlying data are admissible into evidence" and is consistent with South Carolina case law. Adamson v. Marianne Fabrics, Inc., 301 S.C. 204, 391 S.E.2d 249 (1990); Zemp Constr. Co. v. Harmon Bros. Constr. Co., 225 S.C. 361, 82 S.E.2d 531 (1954); Crowley v. Spivey, 285 S.C. 397, 329 S.E.2d 774 (Ct. App.1985); Butler v. Sea Pines Plantation Co., 282 S.C. 113, 317 S.E.2d 464 (Ct. App.1984). It should be noted that the case of Peagler v. Atlantic Coast Line R.R., 234 S.C. 140, 107 S.E.2d 15 (1959), is inconsistent with these prior cases and has been effectively overruled.

Case Law

"Demonstrative evidence includes items such as a photograph, chart, diagram, or video animation that explains or summarizes other evidence and testimony. Such evidence

has secondary relevance to the issues at hand; it is not directly relevant, but must rely on other material testimony for relevance. Demonstrative evidence is distinguishable from exhibits that comprise 'real' or substantive evidence, such as the actual murder weapon or a written document containing allegedly defamatory statements."
Clark v. Cantrell, 339 S.C. 369, 383, 529 S.E.2d 528, 535 (2000)

" '[T]he standard for merely showing or exhibiting demonstrative evidence ... would not be higher than the standard for actually admitting demonstrative evidence.' *Davis v. Traylor,* 340 S.C. 150, 156–57, 530 S.E.2d 385, 388 (Ct.App.2000). 'The trial court has broad discretion in the admission or rejection of evidence and will not be overturned unless it abuses that discretion.' *Id.* at 157, 530 S.E.2d at 388. 'To warrant a reversal based on the admission of evidence, the appellant must show both error and resulting prejudice.' *Conway v. Charleston Lincoln Mercury Inc.,* 363 S.C. 301, 307, 609 S.E.2d 838, 842 (Ct.App.2005). '[C]ounsel may use a blackboard during jury argument to illustrate points that are properly arguable or to bring to the jury's attention facts or figures properly revealed by the evidence.' "
Gibson v. Wright, 403 S.C. 32, 37–38, 742 S.E.2d 49, 52 (Ct. App. 2013)

RULE 1007
TESTIMONY OR WRITTEN ADMISSION OF PARTY

Contents of writings, recordings, or photographs may be proved by the testimony or deposition of the party against whom offered or by that party's written admission, without accounting for the nonproduction of the original.

Note:

This rule is identical to the federal rule. The case law has not previously recognized any limitation on the form of the statement or admission which can be used. Gardner v. City of Columbia Police Dep't, 216 S.C. 219, 57 S.E.2d 308 (1950). Therefore, this rule may be somewhat narrower since it limits the statements or admissions which can be used to those contained in testimony, deposition or written admission.

Case Law

"Rule 1007 allows the proof of the contents of a writing, recording or photograph by the deposition or testimony of a party opponent, without having to account for the nonproduction of the original. This is another form of secondary evidence."
Lorraine v. Markel Am. Ins. Co., 241 F.R.D. 534, 576–77 (D. Md. 2007)

"Because Rule 1007 so seldom is used or discussed in cases, most lawyers are unaware of it. However, given the frequency with which deponents are asked questions about the content of writings, recordings and photographs, it is prudent to

remember that if the deponent is a person whose testimony would qualify as an admission under any of the five varieties recognized by Rule 801(d)(2), then the deposition testimony may be admitted to prove the contents of the writings, recordings and photographs described. The same is true for written responses to Fed.R.Civ.P. 33 and 36 discovery that asks for a description of the contents of a writing, recording or photograph. The need is obvious, therefore, to insure that any characterization of the contents of a writing, recording or photograph that could fall within Rule 1007 be accurate."
Lorraine v. Markel Am. Ins. Co., 241 F.R.D. 534, 582 (D. Md. 2007)

RULE 1008
FUNCTIONS OF COURT AND JURY

When the admissibility of other evidence of contents of writings, recordings, or photographs under these rules depends upon the fulfillment of a condition of fact, the question whether the condition has been fulfilled is ordinarily for the court to determine in accordance with the provisions of Rule 104. However, when an issue is raised (a) whether the asserted writing even existed, or (b) whether another writing, recording, or photograph produced at the trial is the original, or (c) whether other evidence of contents correctly reflects the contents, the issue is for the trier of fact to determine as in the case of other issues of fact.

Note:

This rule is identical to the federal rule. It has long been held in this State that a question as to whether to admit a document under the best evidence rule is addressed to the discretion of the trial judge. Shirer v. O.W.S. & Associates, 253 S.C. 232, 169 S.E.2d 621 (1969); Vaught v. Nationwide Mut. Ins. Co., 250 S.C. 65, 156 S.E.2d 627 (1967); Drayton v. Industrial Life & Health Ins. Co., 205 S.C. 98, 31 S.E.2d 148 (1944); Sample v. Gulf Refining Co., 183 S.C. 399, 191 S.E. 209 (1937); Atlantic Coast Line R.R. v. Dawes, 103 S.C. 507, 88 S.E. 286 (1916); Leesville Mfg. Co. v. Morgan Wood & Iron Works, 75 S.C. 342, 55 S.E. 768 (1906); Wayne Smith Constr. Co., Inc. v. Wolman, Duberstein, and Thompson, 294 S.C. 140, 363 S.E.2d 115 (Ct. App. 1987). There are no cases discussing the role of the trier of fact in this area.

Case Law

"The final rule in Article X of the Federal Rules of Evidence is Rule 1008. It is a specialized application of Rule 104(b)—the conditional relevance rule—and sets forth what must happen when there is a dispute regarding whether there ever was a writing, recording, or photograph, or when there are conflicting versions of duplicates, originals, or secondary evidence offered into evidence. In such instances, as in Rule 104(b), the jury decides the factual dispute. Fed.R.Evid. 1008 advisory committee's note."

Lorraine v. Markel Am. Ins. Co., 241 F.R.D. 534, 577 (D. Md. 2007)

Article XI. Miscellaneous Rules

RULE 1101
APPLICABILITY OF RULES

(a) Courts and Judges. Except as otherwise provided by rule or statute, these rules apply to the courts of South Carolina. The term "judge" in these rules includes justices of the Supreme Court; judges of the Court of Appeals; judges of the circuit, family, probate and municipal courts; magistrates; masters-in-equity; and special referees.

(b) Proceedings Generally. These rules apply generally to civil actions and proceedings, to criminal cases and proceedings, and to contempt proceedings except those in which the court may act summarily.

(c) Rule of Privilege. The rule with respect to privileges applies at all stages of all actions, cases, and proceedings.

(d) Rules Inapplicable. The rules (other than with respect to privileges) do not apply in the following situations:

> **(1) Preliminary Questions of Fact.** The determination of questions of fact preliminary to admissibility of evidence when the issue is to be determined by the court under Rule 104.

> **(2) Grand Jury.** Proceedings before grand juries.

> **(3) Miscellaneous Proceedings.** Proceedings for extradition; preliminary hearings in criminal cases; sentencing (except in the penalty phase of capital

trials as required by statute), dispositional hearings in juvenile delinquency matters, or granting or revoking probation; issuance of warrants for arrest, criminal summonses, and search warrants; and proceedings with respect to release on bail or otherwise.

Note:

Except for subsections (a), (b), and (d)(3), this rule is identical to the federal rule.

In subsection (a), the federal rule has been amended by adding the phrase "except as otherwise provided by rule or statute." See Note to Rule 101. Further, the phrase "courts of South Carolina" replaces the list of courts in the federal rule, and the term "judge" is modified to include all levels of the unified judiciary. These changes emphasize the fact that these rules are applicable to all levels of the unified judiciary.

Subsection (b) indicates that these rules apply generally to all civil and criminal proceedings except for summary criminal contempt. This exception is consistent with the relaxed procedural requirements for the imposition of summary contempt. Cf. State v. Weinberg, 229 S.C. 286, 92 S.E.2d 842 (1956).

Regarding subsection (c), no South Carolina authority has been found to support the proposition that the rules of privilege remain applicable even if the other rules of evidence are inapplicable.

Regarding subsection (d)(1), no South Carolina authority has been found regarding this proposition.

Subsection (d)(2) is consistent with the case law in South Carolina. See State v. Williams, 301 S.C. 369, 392 S.E.2d 181 (1990) (the validity of an indictment is not affected by the character of the evidence considered by the grand jury and, if valid on its face, the indictment may not be challenged on the ground that the grand jury acted on the basis of incompetent evidence); State v. Williams, 263 S.C. 290, 210 S.E.2d 298 (1974) (a grand jury indictment is not subject to dismissal on the basis that it was founded upon hearsay evidence).

To be consistent with the terminology used in this State, the phrase "preliminary hearings" in subsection (d)(3) replaces the phrase "preliminary examinations" in the federal rule. In addition, the phrase "dispositional hearings in juvenile delinquency matters" has been added to subsection (d)(3). Although no cases have been found regarding the application of the rules of evidence to extradition proceedings, subsection (d)(3) is generally consistent with prior law in this State. See State v. Dingle, 279 S.C. 278, 306 S.E.2d 223 (1983) (rules concerning hearsay inapplicable in preliminary hearings); State v. Franklin, 267 S.C. 240, 226 S.E.2d 896 (1976) (before imposing a sentence, judge may appropriately conduct an inquiry largely unlimited either as to the kind of information he may consider or the source from which it may come); State v. Sullivan, 267 S.C. 610, 230 S.E.2d 621 (1967) (a search warrant may be issued on an affidavit even when the affidavit is based on hearsay statements); State v. Hill, 5 S.C.L. (3 Brev.) 89, 6 S.C.L. (1 Tread.) 242 (1812) (the court may hear and consider affidavits when determining whether to admit a defendant to bail). However, as to probation revocation, the rule may constitute a change in the law. See State v. White, 218 S.C. 130, 61 S.E.2d 754 (1950) (hearsay rules applied in review of probation revocation).

Case Law

"We are not concerned with balancing prejudicial impact with probative value when reviewing evidence used in the sentencing phase of a non-capital crime because evidentiary rules are inapplicable in a sentencing proceeding."
State v. Hutto, 356 S.C. 384, 389, 589 S.E.2d 202, 204 (Ct. App. 2003)

RULE 1102
AMENDMENTS

Amendments to the South Carolina Rules of Evidence may be made by the South Carolina Supreme Court.

Note:

This is the federal rule modified to apply to South Carolina.

RULE 1103

TITLE AND EFFECTIVE DATE

(a) Title. These rules shall be entitled South Carolina Rules of Evidence, and may be cited by rule number and the letters SCRE, i.e., Rule ____, SCRE.

(b) Effective Date. These rules shall become effective September 3, 1995.

Note:

The language of subsection (a) is based on Rule 85(a), SCRCP. The federal rules do not contain a counterpart to subsection (b).

Made in the USA
Columbia, SC
22 February 2021